HOW TO LOSE FRIENDS
And Other Social Graces

HANS LEHMANN

Dear Robert + Jane —
Lillian has a
book.
    I have a book.
Now it is your
turn.

                Love
                Hans Lehmann

PARK PLACE PUBLICATIONS
PACIFIC GROVE, CALIFORNIA

HOW TO LOSE FRIENDS
And Other Social Graces

Hans Lehmann

Cover art by Eldon Dedini
Book design by Patricia Hamilton

Library of Congress Control Number:
2001091868

ISBN 1-877809-90-x

Printed in the United States

First Edition July 2001

This book is dedicated to
Wera, Walter, Leni, Arthur and Klaus.
Their love, wit and wisdom have
nourished me throughout the years.
THANKS.

Foreword

We all have our stories, and these are some of mine – the mischievous ones. All tales are true, and I have recorded them to the best of my recollection. I have, however, altered the names of many individuals and places in order to protect the innocent. In no instance did I wish to disparage any person or place.

To me, life has always proved exhilarating and fortuitous. I have felt blessed at every turn and hope the reader relates to these adventures in a similar manner.

I wrote most of the stories in chronological order. In some exceptions, I used flashbacks or changed the time frames.

I would like to thank the many friends who helped me publish this book. Foremost is Eldon Dedini, who drew the enticing cover and to whom I am especially grateful. I also am extremely indebted to Peggy Schissell and Debbie Sharp, who spent innumerable hours in proofing and editing my manuscript. Many friends also encouraged me to write these vignettes; in particular Lillian Evans and Gene Allen, who led the way by writing their own memoirs. And I thank the many individuals who graciously reviewed and critiqued my book on the back cover.

Finally, I want to thank Patricia Hamilton for her invaluable aid and logistical support in helping me publish and market this book. And to Gary M. Russell for making me look so good in his photo.

Hans Lehmann
Carmel-by-the-Sea, California

Contents

I

Albanian Straw

"EITHER REPACK, OR WE DUMP," THE CUSTOMS OFFICIAL somberly advised us. He referred to our numerous cartons of china and other items, packed meticulously in Albanian straw. "No foreign straw in the United States," or so he declared. We repacked.

In this manner, we arrived at Ellis Island. The year was 1939. We were a family of four: my father and mother, my nine-year old brother and I, who was seven.

All of us had been born in Germany. Because of Hitler and our Jewish heritage, we left that country in 1935. We eventually moved to Albania, where our father, a neuro- surgeon, accepted the position of surgeon in chief and private physician to King Zog of Albania. Now, four years later, Albania proved just as troublesome, and we elected to continue our flight.

This must have been a very difficult decision for my parents. My father often remarked that Albania gave him the most challenging and rewarding years of his life. Challenging, because of the countless obstacles he encountered; rewarding, because of his grateful patients, many of whom never had seen the insides of a hospital before and often rode donkeys for days in order to get there.

As primitive as Albania was, there was another side to it. We lived on this opposite side, in opulent surroundings, complete with a large house and staff and an extremely active social life.

For my brother and me, our daily existence meant home schooling with Irmgard, our beloved and attractive tutor, private riding lessons, and fancy parties, wherein we donned our bright red bell-boy uniforms or Albanian costumes and opened the front doors.

One afternoon, we decided to run away from home. Irmgard had asked us to wait outside a small store while she went in. In that interim, we decided to take off; perhaps, because we felt our life seemed too routine. In any event, when Irmgard came out, we had disappeared. Naturally she feared the worst, assumed that we either had been kidnapped or harmed, and was absolutely besides herself. Meanwhile, we scampered through the back streets and alleys of Tirana, totally oblivious to any concerns we might have caused.

After an absence of a few hours, we became hungry and decided to return home. Our father had raced home from work, and Irmgard and Mom seemed most distressed. Our return proved very bitter-sweet. On the one hand, Irmgard, Mom and Dad were thrilled to have us back. On the other hand, they also were livid and now engaged in a heated discussion about our proper punishment.

For the first time in our lives we were roomed and not allowed to open the front doors for a large reception that evening. Even this punishment was short lived. Many guests proceeded to sneak upstairs with cookies and cake in hand, while poor Irmgard remained in her room, sick and thoroughly despondent about the entire ordeal.

Shortly thereafter, primarily because of the enormous tensions mounting throughout Europe, our parents decided to leave Albania. Irmgard elected to remain in Europe. With bitter tears, we parted company.

Fortunately, our parents managed to secure United States visas. Unbeknownst to us, our boat was also the last ship to leave Albania. The Italians invaded two days after we sailed, and the boat almost left without my father. He had been at the hospital, where the queen was delivering her first baby. Luckily, a

Viennese specialist took over shortly before the boat left. Our father caught our ship, the baby was delivered, and the royal family escaped to Yugoslavia.

I don't remember much about that voyage, except for three bewildering incidents. First, I climbed on an electric horse by myself, turned it on high and was unable to turn it off. Luckily, an unknown savior entered the gym.

The second problem involved an unscrupulous Englishman, with but one good eye. He shut his bad eye, placed his hand in front of his face, and extended his closed fist towards my brother and me. As we held our breaths, he slowly opened his fist and exposed a most realistic-looking fake eye. Shortly thereafter, our mother found us, just as we were attempting to dislodge our own eyeballs in front of the mirror.

The third problem was the weather. We ran into some ferocious storms. At times almost everyone got seasick. Our cabin steward became so disconcerted that she refused to clean anything up. Rather, she called on a poor assistant named Campbell. "Campbell, do this." "Campbell do that." And "Campbell, do everything else." I don't remember ever having seen this phantom, but I never forgot his name.

In the midst of episodes like these, we immigrated to the United States. My father spoke English fluently. My mom spoke it quite well. Neither my brother nor I understood a word. We also wore short pants, especially annoying since all of our peers wore long pants. In addition, I wore glasses, a novelty which stood out, and both my brother and I were accustomed to keeping our hands on top of the table during meal times. In the United States, we were told to leave them on our laps. All somewhat unsettling for two young boys.

Many years later, I reflected on our family history, a history that included diverse backgrounds, roots and religions.

✦ ✦ ✦

Like our parents, our grandparents came from Germany. Dad's father, Leo Lehmann, was a successful banker, active in

Frankfurt's Jewish community. Dad's siblings, like our father, were able professionals. Our father even considered becoming a concert pianist before he took up medicine.

Mom's parents stemmed from Polish and German roots and Catholic and Protestant backgrounds. Her father, Karl von Kuczkowski, was a German military officer, who traced his Polish heritage to 1170. Mom's mother was a Stollwerck, one of the wealthy German chocolatiers. As such, Mom grew up with a silver spoon, but the depression and cocoa futures virtually bankrupted the Stollwercks and their elegant way of life.

Mom and Dad were married in the German Lutheran church. The year was 1929.

Previously, while living the life of a successful bachelor-physician, our father had engaged a housekeeper-cook. After Mom and Dad married, Mom, who never had learned how to cook, stood in the kitchen and watched every move the cook made. Eventually, the cook came to my father and said:

"Herr Professor, either Mrs. Lehmann stays out of the kitchen or you will have to find yourself another cook."

Our mother wisely realized the importance of a husband's full stomach and subsequently remained out of the kitchen. Only after she arrived in the States, did she learn to cook. Eventually, she became a whiz.

In the United States, our lifestyles changed dramatically. The days of tutor, housekeeper and cook vanished overnight, and our family of four learned to deal with a new and simpler way of life. Suddenly all of us, but especially my brother and I, learned to fend for ourselves.

✦ ✦ ✦

When we landed in New York City, someone gave my brother and me two small stuffed dogs. These were constantly at our sides. Every morning, we ate breakfast in a small Manhattan diner. Here the waitress greeted us with a cheery, "Where are the little doggies?" Those were among the first English words that I remember.

For a few weeks, we made our home in Manhattan. We based ourselves in a small hotel, from where we formulated our plans. But our plans became elusive, and after some indecision we looked towards the West. Many years previously, my father had studied on the East Coast with Harvey Cushing, the famous neurosurgeon, but Dad never had traveled west of the Mississippi. In addition, the San Francisco Exposition was in full swing, and we had good friends in Laguna Beach, California. Why not investigate, my parents thought. And investigate we did.

We packed our most essential belongings and went by train. It was a fascinating journey, especially for my brother and me, who never had seen a Pullman. One night, we were safely tucked behind our curtains in the long Pullman car. At the same time, our heads peered out between the curtain panels at the passing parade of passengers and attendants. Suddenly, we noticed that the curtains across from us began to bulge. Slowly the bulge increased in size and grew larger and larger. Abruptly the curtains then parted, and a lady in her nightgown fell into the middle of the aisle. Apparently she had been combing her hair and was unaware that slowly she was moving backwards. Except for her disposition, she was unharmed. My brother and I amused ourselves for days over this unexpected interlude. In any event, through incidents like this, we reached the West Coast.

My parents wanted to settle in Laguna Beach. Then someone suggested they first drive around the state. They drove north, took one look at Carmel and Mom said, "Let's move here." In this manner, we came to Carmel. Soon we bought a home, joined the Episcopal church and began to settle down.

II

Gray Bun And A Visor

IN CARMEL, WE ATTENDED PUBLIC SCHOOL. THIS WAS not without its hardships. Among other concerns, we had to deal with Miss Bates, a special education spinster, who had been summoned to teach us English. Miss Bates was an elderly lady, with a large gray bun sitting squarely on the back of her head. She always wore a green visor and round glasses. I thought her most irritating and always tried to hide from her. Wherever I hid, she found me, grabbed me by the arm, and dragged me along. Then she made me repeat the same words endless times, and after an hour or so returned me to class, much to the amusement of my fellow students.

I never felt comfortable in that class. Perhaps because of my short pants. Finally, my brother and I encouraged our mother to purchase genuine Levi's. We drove to Penney's, where we found exactly what we were looking for. Well almost exactly. In those days Levi's came in one length only, and everyone rolled up the bottoms. By chance, we walked in on our Mom, as she was preparing to hem our pants. Had she hemmed our pants, we would have skipped class for sure. Fortunately, we persuaded her to roll them up, like the other boys.

We purchased our home in 1941. Soon afterwards, the United States declared war, and enemy aliens weren't allowed to live directly on the coast. Presumably, because of a fear they might contact enemy submarines. We were Germans. Once again, we were forced to move.

My father, not knowing where to go, tacked a map of the United States on a wall, threw a dart, and hit Colorado Springs, Colorado. He always had been resourceful, intuitive and lucky. Now he showed these traits again. We might have landed in the desert.

We rented a car and trailer, packed our belongings and proceeded. Once we had a blow out and the trailer flipped over. Another time my father talked his way out of a speeding ticket. The ticket incident seemed especially intriguing as my father assumed that the black and white car, with red lights blinking and siren wailing, was an ice cream vendor. After my dad finally did stop, he managed to persuade the policeman not to write the ticket.

Two years previously, when we first came to the United States, *The New York Times*, and other newspapers had written lengthy articles about my father and our escape from Europe. Apparently the police officer was a history buff and remembered those articles. Whereas he first assumed that my dad was a "horse doctor," he now engaged my father in deep conversation and eventually relented from writing the ticket.

In any event, we ultimately reached Colorado. We lived in Colorado Springs for a few months, acquired our first bicycles and worked further on learning our English. Meanwhile, other American friends, whom we had known in Albania, graciously suggested we move in with them. They owned a large farm in upstate New York with an empty flat. We took them up on their kind offer and moved back to the East Coast. Later, we rented a home in nearby Ithaca.

Here I attended the sixth, seventh and eighth grades. Those grades seemed especially memorable.

I attended the sixth grade along with Ted Shapiro, Tommy Thompson, Lee Langdon and some others. Ted's family owned the local grocery store, and I remember one Halloween in particular, when he supplied enormous quantities of cider. Unbeknownst to anyone, that cider had turned quite hard. In this manner, we experimented with our first taste of alcohol.

Cigarettes seemed another story. In those days, many people placed small silver cigarette boxes and lighters on their coffee tables. It was easy for my brother and me to pilfer a few cigarettes, go behind our garage and sneak a smoke. We then disguised these infractions by munching a few chocolates, which were supposed to camouflage our odors.

For my brother and me, smoking was not new. A year previously, on the farm, we had rolled our own cigarettes out of corn silk and toilet paper. But those hand rolled ones seemed far less appealing than the real variety.

The sixth grade was memorable in other ways. One morning, after the teacher left the room, I stuck a needle into the protruding fanny of a startled, neighboring student. She sat next to me and often spread herself amply over her desk chair. I was trying to establish whether that part of her anatomy possessed any nerve endings. I quickly found out.

Immediately the young girl chased me around the room, book in hand, while another student manned the door. Finally she hurled the book, hit me squarely in my face and broke my glasses.

For three days she didn't return to class, as she felt she had to pay for the glasses. When she did come back, I gallantly informed her that it really was my fault and that I would pay. And that was the end of that.

Once, Tommy Thompson and I gave his younger sister a stick of hot pepper chewing gum. Much to our chagrin, she refused to spit it out even though huge tears began cascading down her trusting face. Only after she chewed every bit, did she stop crying.

I can't recall how we even got that gum, as gum was almost impossible to obtain. Those were the war years, and many items were very scarce. Gum was one of them.

I do remember a small cigar shop in town that occasionally acquired a box of Fleers Double Bubble chewing gum. In those days, a piece of Double Bubble seemed precious as gold. At least to a young boy.

One day the cigar shop owner let it be known that on the following Thursday, he would sell exactly one hundred pieces of gum. Word spread like fire, and on the designated day a line formed a block long. One piece per customer at a penny apiece. My brother and I stood in that line and managed to acquire the last piece. Not one piece for each of us. One piece for both of us. To share.

We considered a number of options. We might flip a coin. Or, we might cut the gum in half. Or first one of us could chew the entire piece and then the other. We decided on the last possibility. With certain restrictions.

My brother and I had been raised in a very sanitary environment. Not only was our father a physician, but also our mother, and therefore we felt that this particular piece of gum needed to be sterilized. Boil it we thought, and boil it we did.

I don't know how many individuals ever have dropped a piece of gum into their mom's best pot filled with boiling water. If they did, they would know the result. The gum immediately disintegrates and attaches itself messily and thoroughly all over the insides of that pot. The pot becomes impossible to clean, and the gum is surely impossible to chew. In this manner, we finished off the last piece of Double Bubble and my mom's best pot.

Another memorable event from those years was the time I was shot at. Not with a bullet, but with bb's. One afternoon, a group of us gathered after school. Somebody produced a bb gun and began shooting at the street lights. When it was my turn, I refused. Not because I felt so righteous. Rather, because I disliked anyone telling me what to do. Even then.

"You shoot," warned one of the other students, "or we'll shoot you." As I walked away slowly, bb's cascaded down the back of my jacket. I didn't run, and I wasn't hurt. I merely felt the sting of the bb's.

I preferred the sting of those bb's to the sting of another junior high hazard, namely dancing school. I had begun taking dancing lessons, and I clearly didn't care for them. Especially the part where I had to dance with every girl, whether I liked her or not.

One young lady in particular caused me considerable consternation. Her hands were always sticky. And holding onto someone's sticky hands was not my favorite form of entertainment. Thus, I made every effort to avoid her. Once, the teacher told me that I should dance with Miss so-and-so during the next record.

"I'm sorry, I can't." I objected. "I have an errand to run."

"You run your errand after the dance," the teacher demanded.

"No, I can't," I insisted, "I'm late already." And with that, I rushed down the stairs and out the door. I was totally unprepared for the consequences. The young lady went home to her father, crying bitterly. He called the dance teacher. She called my father. And my father spoke to me.

The next dancing session, I meekly returned and danced with the student, sticky hands and all.

Many other events occurred in those years, but I only remember a few. A couple of arguments. Crushes I had on various girls. Orange slices my mom used to peel for me as soon as I came home from school.

Once, I almost landed in jail. Anyway, I thought I would land in jail. I threw a snowball at a passing car. The driver's window was open, and the snowball hit him in the face. He slammed his car to a halt and quickly jumped out. I tried to race away, up a small knoll. The incline was wet and slippery, and before I reached the top, the driver grabbed me.

"Young man," he shouted, as he picked me up and vigorously shook me, "Do you want to go to jail for the rest of your life?" I didn't.

Soon after, he put me down and returned to his car. That man did me a big favor. I never threw another snowball, at least not at a moving vehicle.

Shortly after this incident, World War II was over, and we returned to our home in Carmel. My parents had rented it to our aunt and uncle, who were allowed to remain on the coast. They had been friendly aliens, whereas we were not. My aunt and uncle were friendly aliens, due to a strange set of circumstances.

Many years previously, when in his thirties, my paternal grandfather, Leo Lehmann, had immigrated to the United States. In 1882, he even became an American citizen.

Shortly thereafter, he returned to Germany for a vacation and fell in love with my would-be grandmother, Emma. She had no intention of emigrating. They remained in Germany, where they raised their family. Leo had lost his German citizenship when he became an American citizen. As he didn't return to the United States within five years, he also lost his American citizenship. He became stateless, as did all of his children.

My father took a professorial oath and by so doing became a German citizen. My dad's siblings discovered if they purchased land in Liechtenstein, they became Liechtensteiners. When the war broke out, my aunt and uncle were Liechtensteiners, and as such were friendly aliens. We were not. They remained in Carmel, while we moved east.

Now that the war was over, our parents returned to their home in Carmel. My brother and I did not attend Carmel High. Our parents felt we had attended too many schools and acquired too little education. With generous financial aid from our aunt and uncle, our parents enrolled us in the Webb School for Boys, a private boys' school in Claremont, California.

III

There's Glue In His Shoe

THE NIGHT BEFORE SCHOOL BEGAN, OUR PARENTS, MY brother and I, stayed at the Claremont Inn, a rustic and popular hotel in the center of Claremont.

In the morning, the Inn's dining room seemed virtually deserted, except for an imposing dowager and her bespectacled son. They sat at one end of the cavern-like dining chamber, and our family at the other.

"Do you think he is going to Webb?" my brother whispered in my ear.

"I hope not," I replied.

As if they heard, both mother and son peered in our direction. Soon the boy arose and came towards our table.

"My name is Jackson Thompson," he ventured, "and my mother wondered whether you two boys also might be going to Webb." My brother and I cringed and desperately wanted to crawl under the table.

"Why yes," my mother pleasantly replied. "How nice of you to ask. I am Mrs. Lehmann, this is Dr. Lehmann, and these boys are Klaus and Hans." My brother and I choked. Then, with clammy handshakes, we introduced ourselves first to Jackson and then to his mother. Neither my brother nor I were very pleased by this turn of events, but we had little choice.

Two hours later, we entered the actual grounds of Webb and immediately observed our new acquaintance walking briskly across the campus, violin case in hand. That was our first introduction to Webb. Eventually Jackson and I became good friends. We even shared a horse. But that's another story.

Immediately, we were assigned rooms. I had been there but a few days when I heard a loud knock at my door. I opened it and discovered a group of noisy students standing outside. One seemed especially upset.

"There's glue in my shoe," he yelled, as he extended a pair of shiny white and brown saddle shoes. "There's glue in my shoe, and they say you did it," he repeated, focusing all of his attention on me. Some of the other students nudged each other. Two smirked knowingly.

I felt weak and thoroughly confused. Not only had I never poured glue into anybody's shoes, but I never had seen this individual in all my life.

Finally I mumbled a feeble no, and between that tiny word and my obvious bewilderment, the noisy contingent continued down the hall. As they left, they shouted a resounding, "You better be right." I became a nervous wreck.

In this unruly manner, began my first week at Webb. I had entered as a freshman, and a young one at that.

The year was 1946. World War II had just finished. The United States of America accepted my parents as citizens, and the Webb School for Boys admitted my brother and me as students. A lot of worldly transitions for a young boy like me, or so I thought.

Every day, the students ate three wholesome meals in Webb's spacious dining hall. At the head of every table reigned a faculty member and his spouse. The instructors always remained at their own tables, but the students didn't. Like clockwork, we moved from table to table. In this manner both students and teachers soon knew each other very well. Since only one hundred and forty students attended school, this progression didn't take long.

The waiters were fellow students. I was one.

Those that cleared their tables first got to eat ahead of their contemporaries and were able to treat themselves to the biggest servings. This was particularly important on those days when we ate ice cream. We always were in a rush to clear off our tables. I remember two incidents in particular which hampered this approach.

Once, I stacked my plates too high. We had eaten baked potatoes for dinner, and as I removed the plates, I placed one plate on top of the other. Each succeeding plate began to lean at a greater angle than the one before. Suddenly, one potato lost its balance, slipped off its perch and down the back of Mrs. Sumner's dress. Mrs. Sumner, more popularly called "Ju Ju," was a very buxom lady who was prone to wearing loose-fitting dresses. The potato lodged itself effortlessly in the back of her dress. Quickly I balanced the other plates with my left hand, reached in with my right hand and retrieved the wayward vegetable. I then made a speedy exit.

The second situation concerned one particular youth who ate more slowly than anyone else. He ate so slowly that we timed his meals. He averaged forty-five seconds per mouthful. The entire task, from initially placing food onto his fork, raising his fork, sticking the fork into his mouth, beginning to bite, methodically chewing the entire mouthful, swallowing and putting a new morsel of food onto his fork, averaged three-quarters of one minute. At first glance, this may not seem long, but if you didn't talk, and he didn't, that length of time became excessive by any standard.

Needless to say, none of the waiters cared to serve at his table. We avoided him like the plague and attempted to change our assignments. I don't know what ultimately happened to him, but I suspect that at the very least he will live to be a hundred and ten.

IV

Der Kaiser

A S WITH ANY ESTABLISHMENT, WEBB HAD ITS OWN hierarchy. I am speaking about the students, not the teachers. The faculty had its own. At the top of the students' hierarchy were the athletes, who lettered in football, basketball, baseball and track. (Lesser sports, like tennis, didn't count.)

Next came the class officers and the honor committee, who were a group of students chosen by their peers, and who seemed particularly blessed with innate leadership qualities. Then came the scholars. Then a group equally renowned, but somewhat infamous, as they were members of the notorious "smoke shack." Then came the rest of us.

I was particularly impressed by the "smoke shack," a small free standing stone building, with its own working fireplace. Anyone accepted to the "smoke shack," had to obtain written permission from his parents allowing him to smoke.

Sometimes one could see tiny wisps of smoke wafting their way out of the chimney, but whether cigarettes or wood caused this smoke one never knew. Needless to say, anyone who was a member of this particular den of iniquity was revered by most of the other students and certainly by me. And if by chance one was not only a member of the smoke shack, but also a letterman, he was just about as close to being God as one might become.

I was not a letterman, honor committee member, leader, scholar, or "smoke shack" member, and only dreamt of how those hallowed individuals actually must have felt.

One of the leaders, whom I remember especially fondly, was Hal Brown Jr. Hal was involved in everything from being chairman of the dance committee to holding down the varsity shot-put slot. He was a big man on campus. At one point he, three others and I even shared a small dormitory called the Field Shack, where I got to know him especially well. In any event, Hal had his fingers in numerous pies. His position as chair of the dance committee is the one that I remember most vividly.

Every year we held six dances. The last dance was a free dance. It was called free because we were allowed to invite anyone we wished. The other dances were all exchange dances, where we were teamed up with a partner from a neighboring girls' school. Weeks before the scheduled exchange dance, those boys who wanted to attend listed their name, height and age. Then Hal and his committee met with the dance committee of the other school, compared statistics and assigned partners. Surely a very benign method of teaming up pairs.

The night of the dance found all Webb boys crammed into its main office, anxiously awaiting the young ladies. Soon two chartered busses drove up. We stared as the young women quickly stepped off the bus and made their way into the powder room. Then we watched them emerge, and the fun began in earnest. For them and for us. Somewhat akin to a lottery.

One by one the dance committee called our names. Depending upon how we felt, we either ran or crawled to the podium. In a few instances, some students managed to circumvent the system entirely. In those cases, they knew their dates beforehand and had worked out a deal with the dance committees. These were the exceptions.

A week before the dance, all Webb students were compelled to attend a detailed lecture on proper dance floor etiquette. Here we were informed of three basic principles which we had to follow.

First, we were not allowed to chew gum. Some years back, one student had and while dancing cheek to cheek managed to entwine his partner's hair with his gum. Nonchalantly, he continued to dance, as he assumed he had plenty of time to untangle the mess. With each succeeding step, he only ensconced the gum more thoroughly in her hair. Finally, at the end of the medley, the gum had to be cut out. So much for chewing gum.

The second lesson was not to stray from a designated thirty-foot-wide path. This path was the road that circled the interior of Webb's grounds, and under no circumstances could we stroll off it during our breaks. Not even by an inch. We were told that the road was patrolled by faculty members and that some instructors even had hidden themselves behind trees. No hanky-panky at Webb, or so Webb intended.

Lastly, we were advised that we had to exchange eight of our twelve dances with other couples. In order to make this rule hold fast, we were required to submit a copy of our dance card to a pre-scribed faculty member before the night of the dance. By this means, the faculty could seek out a student at any moment, look at his dance card, and check if the student was following the rules. If he broke them, he received demerits, was roomed, or something worse, depending on the infraction.

Sometimes, we held dinner dances. These affairs often hap-pened in the spring. And in the spring, we always wore white dinner jackets. I remember this fact well because we always ate spaghetti with tomato sauce for those dinners. To this day I won-der why the menu might not have included a less visible entree. Perhaps the cook needed to maintain a certain budget, or his wife owned the local cleaning establishment. In any event, I always spilled spaghetti liberally over my white dinner jacket.

I remember our last exchange dance especially well. I was a senior, and sometime afterwards my partner invited me to her prom. She did so by writing me a letter, which she sent to Webb. Fortunately the instructor who was in charge of the mail room also was in charge of our dances and was a highly perceptive indi-vidual. Mr. Hooper, the instructor, looked at the letter and knew that the addressee did not attend our school. He also realized that the letter was written by a young woman who attended the same school with which we exchanged our last dance. He then checked the dance roster, noted that I had been her partner, put two and two together and gave me the letter. He felt that the addressee's name sounded too suspiciously like mine. The envelope, you see, had been addressed to Franz Lehar, the famous composer. I guess the young lady had confused our names. It is lucky that she never knew my nick name.

At Webb, I had earned the dubious name of "Der Kaiser." Not because of my German heritage, but rather because of my propensity to expel gas at inappropriate times. Soon I earned the titles of "Der Kaiser" or "Baron von Gas." Even today, I receive an occasional letter addressed to "Der Kaiser." Naturally I discard it immediately.

V

Water Works

WEBB MAINTAINED THREE DORMS: THE UPPER DORM, the lower dorm and the Alamo. The upper and lower dorms were built out of bat and board and had existed for years. The Alamo was rather new, and was built from adobe. It also was built in a large "U" shaped design that resembled a mission and included a bell tower and a spacious courtyard.

The upper dorm was destined for the freshmen and sophomores, the lower dorm for the juniors and the Alamo for the seniors. There also existed the field shack and some other nooks that spread around the campus. Most rooms were double rooms, except for the Alamo, which offered each senior the luxury of his own space.

When I first arrived, I stayed in the upper dorm. My roommate and I shared two cubicles: a small bedroom with two bunk beds, and a tiny study where one barely found sufficient space for two desks. Our main door opened on the inside corridor, as did most others. Rooms were spartan. Occasionally, a bare pipe wound its way down some bleak wall.

One day a particular pipe caused an uproar. Tim Robinson, a fellow student renowned for his creative, albeit mischievous prowess, realized his room's pipe also served as a hot water conduit. Why shouldn't he place a spigot into his pipe and thus avoid the early morning washroom queues? After some thought, he bored a small hole in his pipe. When he withdrew his drill, all hell broke loose. Numerous gallons of hot water began gushing out

under enormous pressure. Tim turned his curtains into tourni-
quets, but to no avail. He then attempted to sweep the oncoming
tide of hot water out of his room. That also didn't work. Soon
every dormer joined him in trying to sweep the steaming hot
water down the hall. All with little success. The gushing water
produced a small flood.

Finally Webb turned off its water at its primary source, a
quarter of a mile distant. Tim received a very stern rebuke and
was roomed for months. Nor did he ever obtain his personal hot
water faucet although he surely found himself in plenty of hot
water. Once I almost found myself in my own batch of hot water.
Luckily, I never was caught.

Among other duties, we were responsible for keeping our
rooms neat, our beds tidy and so forth. Faculty wives made regular inspections, peeked under the beds and performed their work
in a perfunctory manner. Under our beds, we kept personal
belongings such as tennis rackets, suitcases and laundry cases.

Laundry cases were elements from a bygone era, but they
seemed essential in 1946. Each student owned his own laundry
case, complete with reversible address labels. All of us had
brought a pre-described wardrobe to Webb. So many white shirts,
underwear, socks, bathing trunks, tennis shorts, a blazer and so
on. Once a week, we grabbed the dirty laundry, stuffed it into our
laundry case and sent the laundry home. Our mothers washed the
items, reversed the address labels and sent the clean laundry
back.

My mom was especially kind, as she always included a box of
chocolates in every case of returned laundry. I placed these chocolates in a small glass jar squarely on my desk. Time and again, I
left my room and returned a few hours later, only to find the jar
empty. I suspected one student, but didn't know how to stop the
theft. Then I did something rather foolhardy. I obtained two boxes
of Ex-Lax and carefully and methodically scraped off all the let-
tering. Then I broke the tablets into small pieces and placed them
in my glass jar.

The next day, most of my chocolates disappeared once again.

But this time the distrusted individual didn't attend any classes. In fact, he missed classes for three days in a row. I never told him what I had done, nor did he ever suspect my ploy. After that, my chocolates remained undisturbed. And fortunately for me, nobody seemed the wiser.

VI

The Faculty

A S WITH ANY EDUCATIONAL INSTITUTION, THE faculty seemed of prime importance. At the head sat Pappy Webb, the headmaster. Pappy had founded the school shortly before the depression and somehow, by a combination of amazing luck, stamina, determination, fortitude, and a host of other skills, managed to build it into a first class private secondary school.

In 1946, when I first arrived, Webb School already had acquired a formidable reputation. Pappy was a very religious man who spoke in a strong and compelling southern drawl and personally interviewed every student and his parents before he accepted them. Most students followed Pappy's guidelines.

Every morning we marched up to the chapel and listened to a short, non-denominational program. When Pappy spoke, which was often, he would beguile us with his personal stories; generally humorous and always meaningful. How he started the school with no funds. How he felt the faith. How he proposed to his wife. How he despised the use of certain words, like "folks," when used improperly. The importance of being honest. (We signed an honesty pledge after every examination, and we nurtured an honor committee.) The courage of ones convictions. The will to become a law abiding citizen. The desire to rise above the fray. And on. Each speech seemed unique.

One of my favorite memories of Pappy and his wife lacked a moral, unless it was the importance of keeping boys happy on their birthdays. The Webbs lived in a beautiful stone structure at the entrance to the campus. Whenever a student celebrated a birthday, he was allowed to invite a small group of his friends to the Webbs for a birthday party.

At the appointed time, we entered the Webbs' lovely home, sat in their paneled dining room and always received the same treats around a large table. A big cake. Plenty of ice cream. And endless bottles of Coca Cola.

At some point, Pappy and Mrs. Webb would leave the dining room, and immediately we filled our coke bottles with ice cream, shook them up and attempted to hold down the top of the bottles with our thumbs. Of course this proved impossible, and soon the ice-cream-filled coke exploded and sprayed all over the ceiling. I still can see that ceiling, inundated with innumerable Coca Cola stains that had formed over the years. But what fun we had!

Ramsey Harris was another favorite teacher. Mr. Harris was born in Burma and spoke in a very articulate manner. He taught English and also drew. He would draw pictures around his lessons in order to demonstrate a particular point. Sometimes he drew cartoons of "Herbert the Ant." At other times, he drew two huge cliffs and wrote the word "all" on one and "right" on the other. To this day, I write "all right" in two words. And he would write the word "receive," and draw the "e" as a big fish, which ate the dot over the "i." In this way we learned how to spell receive. Recently, Mr. Harris celebrated his hundredth birthday.

There were many individuals who lived long years. One, Ray Alf, was another remarkable teacher. He was a diminutive man, who had been an outstanding athlete in his youth, particularly in track. As such, he taught track at Webb. He also hung by his hands from a pipe in his basement biology class, jumped on his desk, jumped off his desk, scratched under his arms and admonished us as follows: "Men, remember the only difference between a man and an ape is his conscience." Since then, I often have wondered who really had the conscience, but I believe it was supposed to be man. In a similar vein, if we ever inquired whether we had a test, Mr. Alf always responded: "Every day is a test of a man's character." And I guess he was right.

Mr. Alf fathered two beautiful daughters, who were his pride and joy and at whom everybody ogled. He also built a remarkable paleontology museum, which still exists, based on the countless trips he took on Easter vacations with his "peccary men." These students spent hundreds of hours looking for old fossils in the Mojave desert. Although I never became a peccary man, I often wished I had.

Another outstanding teacher was Mr. Sumner, "Ju Ju's" husband. He taught the romance languages and scared me to pieces. He wore an imposing moustache, and whenever he became angry, which was often, his moustache began to quiver like the tail of a rattlesnake. Then he exploded.

"Lehmann," he admonished me, "Why did you do that?

"Because I thought...," I would begin.

"Lehmann, don't think, just do," he cut me off, as he slammed his fist on his desk and swept his books off the table and against the wall. Mr. Sumner had a short fuse.

I never liked Mr. Sumner very much until he voted me "best waiter." A friend of mine had peeked over his shoulder, and watched Mr. Sumner give this amazing testimony on his yearly questionnaire.

Even more illuminating, I returned for an alumni day many years later and discovered that Mr. Sumner and I were fraternity brothers. Suddenly we seemed brethren. Within moments, Mr. Sumner invited me into his home for a drink. Immediately, past sins were erased, and we became bosom buddies.

Under the tutelage of able teachers such as these, I managed to graduate. Maybe not quite magna cum laud. Not even with laud. But I did receive my diploma, which seemed the essential part. With this invaluable piece of paper in hand, I entered the University of Colorado.

Colorado seemed far enough away from home. I also could ski and drink beer at the age of 18. In addition, two classmates from Webb attended. Most importantly, Colorado had accepted me.

VII

College Daze

MY FOUR YEARS AT THE UNIVERSITY OF COLORADO passed far too quickly. From dormitories, to fraternity houses and apartments, my college years proved unusually hectic. It was a continuous challenge for me to remain in school. For someone who rarely tasted beer, who grew up in a strict environment, who went to a boys' boarding school and hardly dated, the University of Colorado seemed a never-ending dream come true.

It was here that wine, women, and song did their very best to get me expelled. After the first semester, I was placed on scholastic probation, where I remained until my final semester. Somehow, I had become too attuned to my new environment.

Once my dad even sent me a concerned letter, enclosing some "C" tablets. Supposedly each tablet "contained more concentration, much more work, much sleep, and less fun." He instructed me to take three a day. "After breakfast with coffee; after luncheon with water; and after dinner with beer." Signed, Walter Lehmann, M.D. He became increasingly frustrated with the constant barrage of pink slips that he and my mom received from the Deans' office. The "C" tablets did little good.

At Colorado, we celebrated TGIF afternoons. ("Thank Goodness It's Friday.") Always on Fridays, but on many other occasions, as well. We gathered at "The Tug," known officially as Tulagi's. Here we indulged in many pitchers of low-alcohol beer. After one such event, I barely made it in time to a sorority house, where I had signed up to be a substitute hasher. Mrs. York, the house mother walked into the kitchen at the exact moment I was showing off my juggling prowess, and had just broken two plates. She fired me immediately. She had a very wry sense of humor.

Another time, the Dean of Men asked that I see him. Supposedly, my roommates and I had once kept certain young women out after hours. Actually, the entire scenario was a bit more complicated than that. Although we had been with them that evening, we also had brought them back to their dormitory, minutes before midnight, which was the proper time of curfew. Therefore, in a literal sense, we hadn't kept them out all night.

What the Dean didn't appreciate was the fact that after we had returned them to their dormitory, three of us subsequently placed a ladder under their window and then brought these same ladies back to the sanctuary of our apartment. Fortunately, after considerable discussion and many fearful moments, the Dean let me off the hook with a very stern warning.

Another time, I felt that if I owned a vehicle, I would study more diligently. Furthermore, I decided that the only way I could get a car would be to convince my father to extend me a loan.

I knew a lady from Texas with a marvelous Southern drawl. I became so smitten with her drawl that I assumed my father would be just as taken. And so I persuaded her to call him and suggest to him that if I didn't have a car, I might get pneumonia. I assumed that once he heard her intoxicating accent, my father would be swayed into immediately understanding my predicament. He wasn't.

Not only was he not smitten, he also couldn't understand her accent, thought that she was a nurse from the hospital and I was in bed with double pneumonia. Only after I picked up the phone and repeatedly told him the entire story, slowly and clearly, did he comprehend. But he was not amused. Nor did he understand the necessity of my acquiring a vehicle, and certainly not then. It was much, much later before he relented.

I joined a fraternity, went through pledging and sought the birth and death dates on specific tombstones which lay in the Boulder cemetery. I performed this task as part of Hell week, along with locating two quarts of chewed chewing gum. Eventually, I became an active member. Life seemed a lark, and I flowed along with the tide, as did many others.

In my sophomore year, two gregarious gentlemen drove in from Los Angeles with California license plates. One owned a brand new and very shiny metallic green Oldsmobile filled with camera equipment. Outside of Boulder, they stopped at a sign shop and had gold signs stenciled carefully on each front door, "MGM Talent Scout."

Before their ruse unraveled, they 1) secured the names, statistics and telephone numbers of most freshmen women, 2) sold that same list to anxious suitors, 3) received free passes to the local movie theater and 4) received permission to park their car on the 50 yard line during football games. These two gentlemen were unusually glib, and as they pledged the same fraternity that I did, I got to know them very well.

In any event, I took only a passing interest in my classes and forgot the content of most of them. One I do remember. That was a class in Financial Management, which was taught by John Thomas. He was a marvelous instructor and taught us the importance of obtaining good credit. First, we should take out a short loan of $200. Then we should pay back the entire amount a few months early. A few weeks later, we were supposed to perform a similar task, with a larger amount. And so on. In this manner, we would build up a solid credit rating. Mr. Thomas was nobody's fool.

I should have listened to Mr. Thomas more closely. Instead, I generally spent my entire month's allowance within a few weeks of receiving it. Then I would go to our Student Union, write a check for ten dollars and promptly spend it. A few days later I would write another check for fifteen dollars and deposit the ten dollars. Shortly thereafter, I wrote a check for twenty dollars and deposited the fifteen dollars, and so on, until the end of the month. At that point, I deposited my next month's allowance.

Banks call this ploy "kiting." Had Mr. Thomas known of my indiscretion, he would have been appalled. But he didn't know, and in those days banks took three days to debit and one day to credit an account. Thus, I had two days of breathing space.

Mr. Thomas celebrated the beginning of each month in a unique manner. He carefully pushed open the large window in our classroom, stuck out his head and took a deep breath of air. Then he loudly proclaimed: "Ah, the second half of my pay-check." Boulder seemed that sweet.

And sweet it was. In fact, it was breathtaking. It was crisp, clean and exhilarating. Partly because of this gaiety, I failed French twice, attended summer school once and needed to take twenty-one units in my final semester in order to graduate. I had one other obstacle to overcome. This problem was my eyesight. For years, I had worn glasses. Sometimes, someone called me "four eyes," or kidded me about my glasses. But I never removed them. I wouldn't, as without my spectacles, I couldn't see. This was before contacts. One day, somebody kidded me once too often, and I removed my glasses. The fact that I couldn't see had nothing to do with my decision. And I didn't put them back on. It seemed that vanity had set in.

VIII

Blind As A Bat

THIS VISION TRAUMA HAPPENED IN MY JUNIOR year. For a year and a half I sat in the last row of a movie, just to prove I could see. I would walk between classes without putting my glasses on. I passed friends. They yelled. I made an apology. And I walked on.

Certainly I wore my glasses to see the black board and to drive. But when in public, I rarely did.

That summer my parents sent me to a psychiatrist. Once a week. The psychiatrist sent me to another one who gave me a Rorschach test. A third interpreted the test. Even with all this attention, I refrained from wearing my glasses.

Then I heard about a system of eye relaxation whereby one never needed glasses again. I began taking lessons in this methodology as well. I saw an instructor twice a week and exercised my eyes every day for ninety minutes. I relaxed my eyes to such an extent that on a few occasions I did receive momentary flashes of clarity. Although these flashes lasted for only a second or two, they seemed a tempting inducement for me to continue my program.

My parents spent so much money on my problem they could have bought my car instead. Still, I refused to wear glasses.

At the end of the summer, I returned to college for my senior year. Once again, I strolled down our walkways, totally oblivious of whom I passed and sat in the last row in movies. The fact that my psychosis remained unchanged didn't help my grades. I couldn't see and wasn't about to make this fact common knowledge. In fact, I became so efficient in covering up, that friends assumed I was more absent-minded than usual. Never did they realize that I was blind as a bat.

Every day I continued my eye exercises. I purchased a special lamp in order to practice in front of it, and I practiced diligently. Although my astigmatism left, my eyes only improved slightly, and my problem continued to plague me.

Then I graduated and a peculiar thing happened. I was inducted into the Army. More importantly, I was issued a uniform, a rifle and a helmet. Suddenly I looked like every other soldier. In addition, the Army lacked women, and I didn't need to be vain. Of course, I did have to see where I was going. No sense in catching a stray bullet just because I couldn't see.

After two years in the service, I received my honorable discharge and went out into the real world. Strangely enough, I no longer harbored any desire to remove my glasses. To this day, I have worn my glasses with ease. Nor have I felt uncomfortable. After all, when push came to shove, who cared if I wore glasses? Certainly, not I. Or anyway, not anymore.

IX

Never Say Never

THE MILITARY PROVED TO BE A PARADISE. IT OFFERED me the opportunity to become a professional goof-off. I received three square meals a day, a nine-to-five job, a uniform, two pair of boots, and I discovered cause for many, many laughs.

Even basic training at Fort Ord didn't faze me. In my first week, we had a platoon leader who had served in the military for twenty-two years. He still hadn't attained private first class. No wonder. He attended a meeting of fellow platoon leaders and returned with considerable information, all wrong. For instance, he told us that on the first day we should lace the shoelaces of both pair of boots "over" the eyelets and on the following day the laces of both pair "under" the eyelets.

We tried to explain that one pair should be laced over, for the odd days, and the other laced under, for the even days. In this manner, the two pair of boots would be differentiated and alternated with each other. Our platoon leader didn't comprehend. Every day we spent unnecessary time in first lacing all four boots over the eyelets, and the next day all four boots under. We did this for about a month until we obtained a new platoon leader.

Then I attended clerk-typing school. Here I learned to type, write orders and perform similar duties. Once I volunteered to take an interpreter's examination. I always had been told never to volunteer, but I decided, never say never. And though I hadn't spoken German in fifteen years, I passed the test with ease. The test was a simple comprehension test. Had the test been on writing, reading or speaking, none of which I was able to do, I would have failed miserably.

Instead, the examination consisted of a few recorded multiple choice questions. "Die Katze ist auf die Bank." I was supposed to decide which was correct: The cat is on the bench, the dog is in the garden, the dog is under the table or the cat is in the kitchen.

I received a grade of 100 and acquired a primary MOS (military occupational specialty) of interpreter. My secondary specialty became that of clerk-typist.

From Fort Ord, I flew to Camp Kilmer, New Jersey, where I embarked on a troop carrier to Bremerhaven, Germany.

On the carrier the fun began in earnest. We found ourselves clustered in large dormitories, awaiting shipboard assignments. These included KP, latrine duty and swabbing the decks. I didn't relish any of these opportunities, even though supposedly a busy soldier was a happy soldier. Instead, I heard the loudspeaker continuously blare out various names.

"Pvt. Jackson Smith, report to the sergeant major's office."

"Pfc. Felix Ovendale, report to the mess hall," and so on.

I thought, why shouldn't I report somewhere too? And what place would be more appropriate than the sergeant major's office? Consequently, I approached the soldier who guarded our door and told him, "They just called out my name." Obviously, I already had realized the importance of the universal "they."

"Who called your name?"

"I don't know. They want me at the sergeant major's office. "

"O.K.," and he let me through.

Finding the office proved a little difficult but I eventually arrived. Once there, I presented myself to the sergeant major.

"They told me you were looking for a clerk typist," I informed him.

"I don't remember asking for a typist," he replied, "but stick around."

For six days I did stick around, as did two of my friends whom I later recruited. We manned the phones and typewriters and even received permission to go to the front of the chow line.

Eventually we reached Bremerhaven.

Here, the fun accelerated. I was placed on a train to Kaiserslautern and then put on another train to Pirmasens. Pirmasens seemed my final destination. I looked at my orders, which clearly stated "to report no later than noon, October 10." October 10 was the following day, and I had learned in clerk-typist's school that we didn't have to report any earlier. I got off the train, grabbed a taxi, found a hotel, ate a delicious meal, and went to sleep. The following morning, I took another train to Pirmasens. Unfortunately, I didn't realize that I had been expected on the previous day's train. Kaiserslautern had called ahead.

When I reached the small headquarters building in Pirmasens, I was greeted by a young clerk.

"Are you Lehmann?" he asked, somewhat bewildered.

"Yes."

"Well, you're AWOL," he replied.

"No. That's not what my orders say."

"Wait until the captain sees you." he quickly answered.

And so I waited.

The next morning, I was summoned into the captain's office. He was a rotund, ruddy-faced individual with a pervasive no-nonsense attitude.

"Lehmann," he bellowed, "you're AWOL."

"That's not what they taught us in clerk-typist school," I insisted.

"Lehmann," he yelled. "This isn't clerk-typist school, this is the Army." He sounded like Mr. Sumner.

"Furthermore," he shouted, "we've got our eyes out for guys like you, and you better watch it. You're in deep trouble, and if you make one bad move, just one, you've had it. You understand?" Each second word was punctuated with a loud obscenity. Of course I understood.

With that, he dismissed me, and for a number of weeks I walked very, very carefully. But time had a way of tempering memories, and after awhile we forgot our initial encounter.

X

Interpreter

MY OFFICIAL JOB, WHICH LASTED FOR EXACTLY three days, was that of being the personal interpreter to our post commander, a lieutenant colonel. His primary task, and therefore mine, was to visit the surrounding villages and to pay courtesy calls on their various mayors or Burgermeisters. Although the colonel might have used a German civilian for these visits, he preferred an American interpreter. Hence, my presence.

On my first day, I tried to tell him that I was born in Germany but had not spoken the language for some time and would need to have a few weeks practice. I got as far as, "Sir, I was born in Germany," when he quickly cut me off.

"I don't care where you were born." That was that.

The next day, we began making our visits.

Unbeknownst to him, the little German I spoke and understood was high German. What they spoke in Pirmasens and the surrounding countryside was a dialect all its own. I hardly understood a word.

And so the Burgermeisters and I would have our own private conversations, in which we smiled and nodded eagerly for the colonel's benefit. Actually, neither side understood what the other was saying, but the colonel didn't catch on.

Three days after I arrived, the local newspaper celebrated its one hundred and twenty-fifth anniversary. This was a very festive occasion, with many speeches, much music and a stand-up comedian. The colonel and his wife, along with six other military couples, sat at a bedecked front table, along with me, their interpreter.

The festivities began with the comedian relating numerous jokes. Once again, I concocted my own stories but often missed the proper punch line. The hall burst out in laughter, while our table was silent. When our table chuckled, the hall was quiet. The colonel asked about this discrepancy, and I explained that Germans' sense of humor seemed different from Americans'. He looked at me somewhat skeptically.

Towards the end, we listened to a brief concert. The first piece was "Zwei Lieder fuer Violine und Klavier." He asked me what a Klavier was, and I explained that it was a piano. The second piece was "Zwei Lieder fuer Violine, Klavier und Cello." We also figured this one out.

Then came "Zwei Lieder fuer Violin, Klavier, Cello und Alt." The colonel asked me what an Alt was, and I told him I couldn't think of its proper name, but that he would recognize the instrument once he saw it. As I spoke, I gestured wildly with both my hands, covering everything from a harmonica to a harpsichord and anything in between. Much to my chagrin, instead of an instrument, I saw a very buxom lady slowly proceed on stage and begin to sing in a vibrant voice. Alt meant alto, and the colonel and I exchanged glances.

That evening turned out to be my last day of interpreting. The next day I was reassigned. My new position was that of message center clerk.

XI

Godsend

THIS NEW POST PROVED A GODSEND. IN THE MESSAGE center I sorted the mail, posted current events and filed unending reams of information. I knew more about conferences, religious retreats and athletic events than anyone else on the base. Thus, I applied for retreats in Berchtesgarten, seminars in Garmisch and tennis matches in Frankfurt. I even started an area tennis team and also began giving tennis lessons to the colonel's daughter. In addition, I received a pass almost every weekend. In short, I lived the life of Riley.

One weekend I neglected to ask for a pass although another soldier and I planned to drive to Mainz. Throwing caution to the wind, we went anyway. He with his pass, I with none.

Mainz proved very invigorating. We wined, dined and danced in beer gardens. We joined a boat cruise and had a wonderful evening. When we finally elected to turn in, it was 4:00 A.M. Rather than spend money on a hotel, we decided to camp out.

We drove into an outlying area, found an open meadow, parked our car and went to sleep. A few hours later we woke up to the sound of voices.

Carefully I put on my glasses, twisted in my sleeping bag and observed many individuals slowly advancing from nearby trees. Each person appeared to be whispering and pointing in our direction. I also heard the sound of police sirens and horns getting closer. Soon, we found ourselves surrounded by three German police cars, one military police vehicle and thirty farmers with raised pitch forks.

Apparently someone had robbed a local bank and escaped in a vehicle that looked suspiciously like ours. Everyone was certain that we were the culprits. In addition, the farmer on whose land we had trespassed complained that we had ruined his grain.

Somehow we were able to persuade the group that we were not the robbers, and I placated the farmer with my best German, which by this time had become pretty good. Finally, everyone left, except for the M.P. He merely asked for our passes.

My friend produced his. I hunted mine feverishly, knowing all too well that I wouldn't find it. The M.P. asked us to follow him to his headquarters.

On the way, we came to a stop light. I jumped out and pleaded my case. He asked when we were leaving Mainz. I told him that afternoon. He suggested that if we left right then, he would let us off the hook. And we left. I certainly didn't want to have another encounter with my company captain.

In the following months I always carried a pass with me and also managed to visit half of Europe. I had such a good time that I almost reenlisted. But then I decided that perhaps, just perhaps, the army featured elements I hadn't yet seen, nor wanted to see.

When my tour of duty was finished, I returned home. No sense in pushing one's luck too much, especially with Uncle Sam. Instead, I turned my attention towards San Francisco.

XII

Never Change Your Barber

A FRATERNITY BROTHER CONVINCED ME THAT I should move into a boarding house. In San Francisco, boarding houses, or residence clubs, seemed omnipresent. They were co-educational, served two meals a day, harbored professionals and seemed the ideal place for newcomers. And so I joined the Lodge. Here I remained for a number of years.

My friend also suggested that if I didn't know what I wanted to do, which was correct, I should go into retailing. Here I would learn business firsthand, be exposed to countless business situations, meet people from different backgrounds of life and decide my future. And so I followed his advice and got a job as a management trainee with The Emporium, a large San Francisco department store. I progressed rapidly and once even interviewed for a prime job within that organization.

This was a position which lead directly to mahogany row, or so I was told, and one that every management trainee arduously coveted. The position was that of managing the New York Buying Office. It also was a position for which the presidents of both the Emporium and Capwells, its sister store, personally interviewed each prospective candidate.

There was only one rub. The president of the Capwells division, in Oakland, possessed a legendary and frightening reputation. Supposedly, he ate nails for breakfast.

I resolved to do everything possible to sway the odds in my favor. Included in my plan were a haircut, a professional shave (my first ever) and a professional shoe shine. I intended to complete all of these tasks in Oakland, which sat across a bay from San Francisco, the morning of my interview. My appointment was for 11:00 A.M. on an auspicious Monday morning.

When I drove to Oakland, I made a horrible discovery. Whereas San Francisco's barber shops were open on Mondays, those in Oakland were closed. And by now, I didn't have enough time to turn around.

Determined to overcome my obstacles, I rushed to the nearest drugstore, purchased a razor and ran to the YMCA.

And then it happened. Caught between a new blade and a nervous disposition, I cut myself badly. Cold water and tissue paper accomplished little, and soon I bled like a stuck pig. To make matters worse, time was running out, and by now I had ruined my white shirt as well.

I hurried into a nearby clothing store, purchased a new shirt, threw it on, polished my shoes with the back of my pants and raced to the interview.

The president exuded authority, appeared in total command and dressed immaculately. Furthermore, he sat behind the glossiest desk I ever saw.

I strode in, extended my hand and attempted to portray myself as an assertive individual. I also lost my balance and planted ten exceedingly moist fingerprints squarely in the middle of his desk.

The president stared and continued to stare at only three objects. He first focused on the middle of his desk, now badly tarnished, then at the remnants of tissue on my face and finally at the noticeable creases on my new shirt.

I didn't receive the appointment. The Emporium's personnel department seemed perplexed. "We do not know what happened," the department told me, "but apparently your interview didn't go very well."

I could have told them that and also my regular barber, after I finally saw him. And I learned a very important lesson. Never, but never, change your barber. Shortly thereafter, I decided to change my job instead.

XIII

Fred Meyer Of California

FRIENDS WARNED ME THAT ONE SHOULD ALWAYS have a new job in hand before quitting the old. But I was young, eager and willing, and one day I gave notice to The Emporium. Much to my dismay, my first day of job seeking turned into a second. The second interview into a third. The third application blank into a fourth. And so on. I became so tired of reciting my background, education and interests, that I began to feel like a robot and acted like one.

What career I really wanted to pursue and how to get there were becoming unimportant issues. Just acquiring a job, any job, became objective number one and this goal turned out to be virtually impossible to attain.

One day I signed up with a new placement agency. This agency had a client who was a German immigrant and who was seeking a young individual to become his factory protege. This gentleman manufactured fire screens and accessories. Most of his workers spoke German and he planned to expand. As I was German and an immigrant and young, I realized that here indeed was a possibility. We set up an interview for the next day.

The following morning, I arrived at a small factory on the outskirts of San Francisco called Fred Meyer of California. Everything seemed quiet, but I located a tiny anteroom in which I sat. My appointment was for 8:30 A.M., and whenever I heard anyone approach, I jumped up.

I waited a few moments when a large man with snap brim

hat, pipe and long over overcoat bounded up the stairs two at a time and confronted me.

"Are you," he bellowed in a powerful accent, "Fred Meyer?"

"No, sir, I am not."

I had made an appointment with Fred Meyer. Many years previously, Mr. Meyer wanted to call his firm "Fred Meyer," period. But another Fred Meyer, a large corporation, existed in Oregon and therefore he decided to become, "Fred Meyer, America's Largest Manufacturer of Fire Screens." That also produced a problem, as numerous manufacturers of fire screens existed that appeared much larger than his firm.

He finally elected to become, "Fred Meyer of California, America's largest manufacturer of *modern* fire screens and accessories." That seemed to be all right. Fred Meyer, you see, possessed plenty of chutzpah.

At any rate, here I sat, waiting for my unknown interviewer while this unknown antagonist accosted me.

"Are you sure you are not Fred Meyer?" my new-found nemesis asked again. And as he did so, he scrutinized me very thoroughly.

"No sir, I am not," I repeated once more.

"Well, if you are not, who is?" demanded my persecutor. Surely I felt stunned. Before I could answer, he suddenly shouted,

"I know you are not, and do you know why?" I was stymied.

"Because I AM Fred Meyer," he blurted out. And with this admission, he marched into the next room and motioned me to follow. As he entered, he pushed aside chairs and office workers like they were straws in the wind. Obviously, he knew where he was going and like a mesmerized duck, I followed.

Fred Meyer's desk and chair seemed very imposing, but he appeared even more so. In fact, with every outburst I began to feel more and more intimidated. First he asked me a series of questions.

"Do you know who Fred Meyer is?" I wasn't sure of my response.

"Well, I know and do you know why?" I sat, fixated.

"Because I AM Fred Meyer."

"Do you know who is the most progressive firm in the United States?" I cringed.

"Well, I'll tell you. It's Fred Meyer of California. And do you know why?" I meekly nodded.

"Because I AM Fred Meyer." With this, he jumped up and pounded the table with his fist.

"And do you know who looks out for its employees more than any other firm?" I was beginning to suspect.

"And do you know why?" By this time I knew for sure.

In this manner, the morning flew by. At the end, Fred Meyer offered me a job. And I took it. I really had little choice. Who in his right mind, (although mine seemed questionable at that point) would have refused? In addition, I had few options.

Fred Meyer turned out to be an innovative, charismatic and industrious individual who started his firm from scratch. He established it in order to find work for himself, his family and his friends, all of whom arrived in the United States without jobs. He was a tremendous salesman and a very shrewd individual.

The next day, I started. I sold fire screens to furniture stores in Redding, sometimes in 100 degree heat and later in Oakland and finally in most of Northern California. The work proved exhausting at times and stimulating at others, and I became a compulsive talking machine. Each day I visited a few old stores, some new ones and made many blind calls.

After eighteen months, the joys of living out of a suitcase began to wane, and I decided to return to college. I applied to the Harvard Business School and miraculously was accepted. I had work experience, good references, reasonable scores on my SATs and had spent over one hundred hours filling in my eight page application form. All of these factors helped, but especially the last.

Fred thought the whole idea crazy.

"Why go to college if you can succeed here," he bellowed.

"Why quit, when you're ahead?" he shouted.

"Who ever learned anything in books, anyway?" he demanded.

"Are you out of your mind?" he yelled.

Obviously, Fred became very displeased. In fact, he fired me, and at once, and so I left. It was many years before Fred and I became friends again. But I will never forget his exuberance and wild enthusiasm.

Licking my wounds at being fired and very embarrassed, I crawled back to the Lodge. It seemed to offer the peace and comfort that I craved at that particular time. It also promised to provide a short interlude before my Harvard venture.

XIV

How To Lose Friends
And Other Social Graces

THE LODGE SEEMED LIKE A HOME AWAY FROM home in more ways than one. It also offered me the opportunity to practice one of my favorite avocations, impetuous behavior.

One evening, after finishing my laundry, I realized that I had failed to wash one sock. This solitary sock now glared at me from the center of my carpet. For many people, one lonely sock would seem of little importance. For me, who disliked the idea of doing my laundry and matching my socks in the first place, one clean sock and one dirty sock seemed too much. I quickly dashed upstairs, saw that the laundry was in use, and casually tossed my sock into the middle of the suds.

I knew the young lady who was washing her clothes and casually told her, "Melody, if you find a spare sock in your laundry, it's mine."

"O.K." she responded. "No problem." And with that, the matter was closed, or so I believed. No such luck.

An hour later, a loud knock on my door awoke me out of my reverie. A very distraught and somewhat hysterical Melody held up seven light blue uniforms.

She had just started a new position and had been washing out her brand new uniforms when in popped my navy blue sock. In moments, her sparkling white uniforms transformed themselves into a bleary blue.

Shocked and at a loss for words, I mumbled a very perfunctory apology.

"You'd better do more than that," screamed a highly agitated Melody. "Those uniforms were my new job."

"What I meant to say," I stammered, "is that I'd be happy to buy you seven new uniforms."

Hearing this offer, Melody showed great relief and indicated she first would try to wash them out with bleach. Miraculously the bleach worked, and the uniforms turned pure white once again. I didn't have to purchase new uniforms, and Melody and I remained friends.

On the other hand, that little episode reaffirmed that doing ones laundry was for the birds. At least for me. It also made me question whether the Lodge really was meant for me. I had gotten into trouble on too many other occasions, especially playing practical jokes.

I remembered my aunt, who always lectured me about my penchant for playing practical jokes.

"Don't you understand," she admonished me, "no one likes practical jokes except the person who plays them?" I never believed her and therefore continued to play numerous jokes on friends, acquaintances and relatives. At one time, I played so many that my poor mother concluded, "Hans, if you continue in this manner, no one will believe you about anything." She may have been right.

My mother made this observation shortly after I dropped an old metal tray full of stainless steel silverware and many metal lids onto the kitchen floor. I dropped this metal tray, which I had concealed, right after I left the dining room, carrying another tray loaded with our best china and crystal.

Needless to say, all the guests believed that the tray of crystal was the one that crashed. My mother didn't appreciate my joke, nor did my father, nor did the guests, although I did hear at least one sigh of relief. I thought the entire episode was a howling success and grinned from ear to ear.

In San Francisco, I carried this unfortunate inclination with me. I had a roommate, Bob, with whom I drove to Yosemite. We assembled our gear, tent and sleeping bags, purchased food and were off.

The first day proved uneventful. The second was different. We decided to hike up Yosemite Falls and filled our knapsack with sandwiches, jackets and medicine kit. For a few hours we hiked up the steep trail that ran parallel to the falls, walking over numerous stone steps, boulders and switch backs.

I carried the knapsack, as it proved very light and I continued to carry it the entire three thousand feet up. Meanwhile Bob often asked if he might carry the pack, but I always turned him down.

Finally we reached the summit, ate our sandwiches, drank our refreshments and took a long nap. Eventually, the weather turned chilly, and we put on our jackets and proceeded back down.

Once again, Bob asked if he could carry the knapsack, but I politely refused. Shortly thereafter, as we walked down the trail, a devious thought crossed my mind. Directly in front of me sat a large and well-rounded rock. It seemed the perfect size for my knapsack and suggested, "Please take me along." Meanwhile, Bob hiked some fifty yards ahead.

I removed my knapsack, opened the flap and carefully inserted the rock. Eventually I caught up with Bob and waited for him to repeat his request. He did.

"Hans, let me carry the knapsack. Please?"

Reluctantly I agreed and removed the pack from my shoulders. I took it off very carefully and helped my friend place it squarely on his shoulders. In that way, he was unable to see the protruding rock. Rather, he "oomphed" a little but gamely straightened up.

In this manner, we proceeded down the trail. On occasion, other hikers looked at us and particularly at Bob and his rock. No one said a word.

Meanwhile, Bob didn't utter a sound either although he had but one thought:

"How could Lehmann carry this pack full, up the hill, when I hardly can carry it empty down?" He gritted his teeth and labored on.

In this fashion we marched some three or four miles. At the bottom stood a small toilet. While I waited outside, my companion went in. Inside, he glanced into a mirror and instantly saw the rock.

Bob became furious. In fact, he became so upset that he easily would have crowned me with his rock, had he found the strength. Instead, he called me every name under the sun and remained bitter for the rest of the day. That evening we finally made up, and we still are good friends.

With another friend, I didn't fare as well. One day I invited a couple to a picnic. These were friends whom I had known for years. Both were German, and he was a successful architect. He also appeared very knowledgeable about many things, including wines. In fact, he loved to boast about his expertise.

I decided to play a little game with him. A small test, you might say. For some time, I owned an old French wine bottle which I used for a candle holder. Why not clean it up and fill it with bulk wine?

This I did, and throughout the meal Alex complimented me on the wine.

"Oh Gretl," he exclaimed to his wife. "This Hans really knows his wines. My, what a wonderful wine," and he savored another sip.

If I had been smart, I would have nurtured this little joke in private. But wisdom never seemed one of my fortes, and at the end of the picnic I spilled the beans.

Alex didn't think my little prank amusing at all. In fact, he became highly perturbed and embarrassed, and so did his wife. And we never did make up.

Another time, at the same residence club, I got into mischief once again. A surrogate aunt had offered me the use of her car during Christmas vacation while she went away. At the time, I didn't own a vehicle.

Her automobile was a Thunderbird, and a brand new one at

that. For two weeks I used it almost every day. At the end of this time, I drove it to a nearby hotel and had it washed, lubed and filled with gas. I planned to pick up the car the next day in order to return it to my aunt.

That night, our residence club gave a small cocktail party and afterwards one of the resident women and I took a short walk. While we walked, we passed by the hotel with the garage.

"I'll tell you what," I suggested to my friend, "why don't you pick out a car, and we'll drive it away." Naturally, she thought I was kidding. I, on the other hand, banked on her choosing the Thunderbird. She did.

I then asked her to wait at the entrance, strolled over to the attendant, paid my dues and drove off. On the way out, I picked up my friend.

"What are you doing," she screamed. "Are you crazy? I thought you were kidding."

"It's too late now," I shrugged, as I drove off.

My partner was not elated. In fact, she became highly distraught. Immediately I pulled to the curb. Again, I had underestimated the consequences of a practical joke. I spent over two hours trying to convince her of the joke, comparing registration papers to my driver's license and attempting to prove that the car's owner lived in Carmel, as I did. I assured her over and over that my aunt lent me the car in the first place. And of course, I apologized innumerable times.

Needless to say, our quiet stroll ended up in an agonizing fashion, and I lost another friend.

With this type of reputation following me, I decided it was time for me to leave the Lodge and move to the east. I had one other item that needed to be resolved before I moved. Two months previously, I had begun a class in self-hypnosis. I always had harbored a fear of dentists and now was going to learn a new panacea.

XV

Mind Over Matter, Maybe

THIS COURSE IN SELF HYPNOSIS WAS MEANT TO assuage any fears I might have of seeing a dentist. My instructor was a Frenchman named Francois le Blanc, who seemed highly regarded in his art. When I inquired whether I could lose my fear of dentists, he waxed enthusiastic. Not only was my idea possible, but definitely achievable. I only needed to desensitize my hands and then transfer this illusion to my lips. In other words, a snap.

Naturally I signed up. Immediately. A nine week course in self-hypnosis might easily relieve decades of fear.

Three weeks later, I learned to put myself to sleep with ease. Under Messr. le Blanc's able tutelage, our class of twelve slowly counted from zero to twenty and then back to zero again. With every count, we fell deeper and deeper into a trance-like stupor.

Messr. le Blanc carefully articulated each sentence.

"You slowly are walking down a staircase, ONE; and your eyelids are becoming heavy, TWO; and the walls are covered in a soft red velvet, THREE; and you are beginning to go to sleep, FOUR; and you want to go to sleep, FIVE; and your eyes are beginning to feel even heavier, SIX"... and so on.

By the time we reached twenty, we felt unusually relaxed. Then we gradually counted in reverse, while our eyelids became lighter with each count. At the point of zero, we began all over again.

Often Messr. le Blanc related numerous stories about the use of self hypnosis. One of my favorite hypotheses was learning how to stop one's veins from bleeding in case of a major accident. Or being able to walk on fire. Or alleviating a skin burn with imaginary ice. The possibilities seemed endless.

At the same time, I began to question our instructor and whether he really was able to hypnotize. I knew I fell asleep. But I doubted whether I ever became hypnotized and felt the other students weren't hypnotized either. But I was game and at every class attempted to desensitize my hands and lips.

One day we discovered nine new members in class. These were prospective students who came to observe.

Messr. le Blanc induced us to sleep and gradually asked us to perform for our visitors. We were going to do minor tricks, such as being glued to a chair or becoming intoxicated from a glass of plain water and so forth.

I harbored suspicions and didn't want to embarrass our instructor. I hoped Messr. le Blanc wouldn't call on me, but he did. Suddenly, he called me to the front of the class and attempted to hypnotize me.

"When Messr. Lehmann wakes up," suggested Messr. le Blanc, "he will untie his shoelaces."

Did I have news for him. I had no intention of untying my shoes. While Messr. le Blanc counted to twenty, I began to daydream. In this dream, I saw a carpeted stairway with a slight bend. In the middle of this bend stood a shiny podium, and in the middle of the podium sat a large book. The book was open. Clearly pulsating from its pages, in bright neon lights, were the distinct words "BULL SHIT, BULL SHIT, BULL SHIT."

When Messr. le Blanc asked me to untie my shoes, I refused. Even worse, after he woke me, he asked why I had refused. In the most diplomatic words I could muster, I explained that I didn't think I was under hypnosis.

"Ah," he proclaimed in a strong accent, "perhaps you feel this entire class is baloney?"

I agreed.

"Perhaps you think that nobody has been under hypnosis?

I nodded.

"Perhaps you think that this whole class was a waste of time and money?

Once again, I said yes. At this point, I was very embarrassed, but what could I do?

"I'll tell you what," Messr. le Blanc answered my thought. "Why don't we put you under hypnosis again and let your subconscious decide?"

This idea seemed fine with me. At least I wouldn't offend the entire class.

Once more, Messr. le Blanc slowly counted to twenty, assuring me that I was falling deeper and deeper into sleep. Whether I was being hypnotized was another question, at least to me.

Finally I heard him call out,

"Subconscious of Messr. Lehmann, please tell us whether or not Messr. Lehmann was under hypnosis." As he spoke, my mind wandered. I daydreamed again, but this time my dream took me beneath a wooden fence. While I strolled, I spied a large giraffe on the other side of the fence, arching its neck and eating. It barely reached the edible leaves hanging far from above.

At that exact moment, I heard the entire class break out in a loud and raucous roar. Then Messr. le Blanc woke me up and smiled in a most knowing and depreciating manner.

Apparently, when the giraffe arched its neck, I nodded my head up and down so vigorously that some students thought I was beginning to convulse. Obviously, Messr. le Blanc had placed me under his hypnotic spell, and the giraffe was my messenger.

Since then, I have accomplished my desensitizing techniques many times and visited my dentist with far less apprehension than before. I learned to go to sleep at the drop of a hat and no longer needed to be concerned with insomnia. I also decided that with these new tools at my disposal, I now was ready for Harvard.

The Harvard Business School may have established a tough reputation, but with my proven ability to sleep at a moment's notice, and thus replenish my energy, coupled with my proficiency at performing self hypnosis, I was prepared. Or so I hoped.

XVII

East Is East

THE HARVARD BUSINESS SCHOOL POSSESSED ONE thing in common with basic training. Everyone started at the same square. Whereas the Army equalized everyone by cutting their hair short, the Harvard Business School made no assumptions whatsoever about students' abilities.

Whether one had been an attorney, a grade A student or a class president, it made no difference. We all were presumed inept and generally failed our first written assignment. If we thought we were smart, we quickly discovered we were not. If we felt we were correct, we quickly found out we were wrong. We had a Heisman trophy winner who wore his letterman's jacket exactly one week. Then he hid it from view.

I saw grown men running desperately in order to post their weekly WAC assignments (written analysis of cases) in time. At exactly 9:00 P.M. on Saturday night, the appropriate mail slot shut down. If you were late by one second, you were docked one grade.

I had a roommate who was a bright engineer from Italy, but with only a fair knowledge of English. His first marketing examination concerned Borden's cottage cheese. He scanned his dictionary for cottage, saw it meant little bungalow and devised a clever marketing strategy for selling cheese that looked like small houses. He failed that test miserably.

Each of our classes was held in a horseshoe-like class room with tiered rows. Anyone might challenge the instructor or vice versa, or any one student might challenge any other. Every day became a verbal free for all, and every case analysis seemed to become a trap. We worked all night in planning our cases and within moments of presenting them would be shot down. As in basic training, every day seemed a day in the trenches.

In this manner, we passed two very intensive years. Work, work, work. Study, study, study. And sleep on occasion. But, we developed numerous skills and learned a lot.

The weekends were different, however. Sundays usually were free, as were Saturday nights, after we had submitted our WAC's. Then there was cause for celebration or a night on the town. Occasionally, we were given brief vacations or holidays. Time permitting, I often turned my attention to New York City, where I visited my brother. Unfortunately, I found myself in a predicament there on at least two occasions.

On the first occasion, my brother had been invited to a party and took me along. We both were broke and made a solemn pact to go home directly after the event. No after-hours drinks or anything more to eat. Not for us.

The party proved to be a delight, with stimulating guests and enough delicacies to whet our appetites, but not enough to fill our stomachs. Then the gathering petered out. Some of the guests continued the festivities at another site and asked us to join them. We declined.

Once outside, we discovered that five guests had already lodged themselves firmly in my car. Although we told them that we had another engagement (a euphemism for being broke) our passengers didn't listen.

"Come and join us," they pleaded. "Just for a minute. We're going to a wonderful little French restaurant. Just for a bite. Nothing fancy. Please join us,"

And like the captive fools that we were, my brother and I joined.

Certainly New York restaurants were a dime a dozen. This particular one seemed no different. It offered a long bar in the front and a small dining room in the back. It also exuded that distinct aroma associated with expensive food. We should have turned at once, but now it was too late. We resigned ourselves to joining the group.

We sat at the very end of a long table and mentioned loudly that we weren't hungry. Then we ordered a cup of coffee and a minuscule slice of cheese cake. Most others ordered pheasant under glass, truffles, a bowl of onion soup and so on. French wine flowed like water.

I remember making numerous calculations as to whether we had sufficient money to pay for our coffee and cake.

Suddenly, a harsh proclamation startled my arithmetic prowess. One of the guests, a man whom I already instinctively disliked, rose noisily, banged his glass and loudly decreed:

"Listen, rather than figuring out who owes what, why don't we simply split the bill by seven and let the men pay for everyone?" There were seven men and nine women present.

Cries of delight greeted this spontaneous announcement. The women, who represented the majority, were thrilled with this plan. Most of the men, who obviously possessed bulging wallets, didn't seem to mind. Only my brother and I acted distraught, and if anyone noticed this fact they didn't seem to care.

I always disliked confrontations, particularly in French restaurants and definitely with my brother's acquaintances. My brother felt the same. We sat like two bricks on a wall and thought of alternative solutions. We could admit to being broke. We could borrow money from someone we didn't know that well. We could refuse to pay. And we lacked credit cards.

Then I had an idea. Why not go to a phone, call a friend who lived nearby and borrow money from him? That way, we would save face. But my friend wasn't home, and I thought of another solution. I would seek a pawn shop and pawn my watch. But there were no pawn shops in that area, and if there had been, they would have been closed. By now, the idea of saving face had obsessed me and the thought of a pawn shop stimulated my imagination. With this thought came a corollary idea. Why not go directly to the horse's mouth? Why not pawn my watch with the bartender? Obviously, my course in Marketing Solutions had taught me something.

With hardly a care, I turned around and briskly headed directly towards the bar. The bartender, a surly-looking individual, scarcely believed his ears.

"Buddy," he exclaimed, "in all my years as a bartender, I never hocked anyone's watch."

"Nor have I," I assured him, while pleading my case.

Surprisingly, either the bartender seemed less surly than I had thought, or he wanted to rid himself of an obvious pest. In any event, and much to my delight, he agreed, gave me some bills and took my watch.

Moments later I returned to my seat, threw a fist full of twenties on the table and handed my brother a note. The message read:

"Don't tell anyone, but I just hocked my watch with the bartender."

My brother almost fell off his chair. Tears of laughter streamed down his face, and the entire table shook. Nobody else saw the note.

The next day I attempted to retrieve my watch. I thought I knew the address, but I didn't. For two hours I strode up and down the upper East Side, desperately trying to locate the restaurant. I never realized that New York City possessed so many French restaurants. Each looked and sounded like its neighbor. Finally, after almost giving up, I managed to reach my goal and soon retrieved my watch.

During the rest of the week, my brother and I ate nothing except peanut butter and jelly. I had my watch, and both my brother and I saved face. But saving face now seemed to be a plague. The following year when I visited my brother again, I encountered another predicament. That time, I didn't fare as well.

XVII

Another Faux Pas

THE NEXT YEAR, WHILE VISITING MY BROTHER, I became involved in such a series of social faux pas, all within moments, that I thought myself impaired. A classmate had invited me to a cocktail party from 5:00 P.M. until 7:00 P.M., which was hosted by his parents. They lived in an elegant Fifth Avenue coop and suggested their son invite a few of his friends. I was one of those privileged guests.

Shortly after I accepted, another classmate invited me to another party at the identical hour, but quite distant. I should have declined the second invitation, but didn't. Never should I have attempted to attend both, as the logistics seemed too cumbersome.

But I decided to go to both, with a definite plan in mind. I would go to party number one at 5:00 P.M. sharp, stay for an hour or so and then proceed to party number two. In this manner, I would kill two birds with one stone. Little did I know that one of those birds would be me, and by making this decision I created my first faux pas.

On the appointed day, I slipped into my best shirt, suit and tie and appeared punctually at 5:00 P.M. in front of my host's door. An astonished maid opened the door and led me into a deserted apartment.

I quickly realized that party number one didn't begin at 5:00, but rather at 6:00. In this manner, I committed faux pas number two.

The maid ushered me into the library.

When I inquired about the hostess, I was informed, "She isn't quite ready yet, sir."

The host?

"He hasn't come home from work yet, sir."

My friend?

"I believe young Mr. so and so is still washing up, sir."

At that juncture, I made my next error. Rather than leave and return later, I decided to stay. For the next forty-five minutes, I sat alone in that library although the maid did come in a couple of times and offered some refreshments.

By the time the three hosts wandered in, I had become a nervous wreck. Then I realized that even had I come at 6:00, I still would have been too early. No other guest appeared until at least 6:30, and in the interim the three hosts and I spent considerable time talking about very little.

I also realized that I fit into these surroundings as smoothly as a square peg in a round hole. I became convinced that my friend's mother thought the same.

By 7:00 P.M., there may have been seventy or eighty guests, each quite articulate and seemingly debonair. I attempted to show the same kind of class. When the maid offered a tray of tiny shrimp, impaled on toothpicks, I took one shrimp and boldly thrust it into a bowl of sauce.

As I withdrew my toothpick, I realized I had lost my shrimp. Then I made my next mistake. Rather than spear another shrimp, I attempted to rescue my original, which by now had sunk.

Time and again I tried, only to come up empty-handed. Meanwhile the maid watched with a mixture of horror and total fascination. By the time I finally succeeded, my shrimp was inundated with sauce. I carefully swallowed the shrimp, threw the toothpick away, and wiped my soiled hands with a handkerchief.

Only then did I realize that the fireplace, in which I had tossed my toothpick, was an empty marble enclosure, meant for decoration only.

Shortly thereafter, the hostess appeared with a solitary toothpick in her hand. Eagerly I located an ashtray and extended it to her.

"Oh thank you," she proclaimed haughtily. "You know, sometimes people throw these into the fireplace." I winced.

I realized that one strange individual should not make much of an impact. But by arriving early, doing little and saying less, I seemed to have made an indelible impression on my hostess. Of this fact, I was certain, and therefore I tried to stay out of her way.

Some time later, she appeared once again. This time, she was preparing to light a cigarette. Like the gallant gentleman that I tried to emulate, I immediately lit a match and flourished it towards my hostess. At that moment, I realized she had placed the wrong end of the cigarette into her mouth. Somehow, my nervous disposition seemed to have rubbed off on her as well.

Once again, a social decision confronted me. Should I pretend nonchalance and light the wrong end, or should I casually advise her of her error? An awkward situation at best.

I decided to pretend nonchalance, lit the wrong end and made a hasty exit. At that point discretion suggested a fast good bye, and by so doing I made my first correct decision of the evening.

I then went to party number two, but it had broken up. And so I returned to my brother's apartment.

The following day, I drove back to Harvard. The Business School may have been difficult, but compared to Manhattan parties, it seemed a snap. Just let me graduate, I decided, and soon. The following semester, I did graduate and shortly thereafter I returned to San Francisco.

XVIII

On The Counter In Taiwan

WITH MY MASTER'S DEGREE UNDER MY BELT, I JOINED Macy's California, a division of R. H. Macy's. In short order I became spellbound by the retailing business.

I began as an assistant buyer in San Francisco, became a department manager in San Jose and a Merchandise Manager in Sacramento. Then I returned to San Francisco as a buyer for cameras, games and trim-a-home. Eventually, I bought for Boys' 8-14 and finally moved to Macy's Monterey, where I became the operations manager and assistant store manager. Wherever I landed, uncommon situations followed.

Once, Macy's sent me to Asia to buy promotional boys' wear.

We were a team of three and represented a number of divisions. At one manufacturer, the three of us argued over which hues we should use in a certain knit shirt. We never reached a compromise and tossed coins. That shirt became a best seller.

On that same journey, we flew from Taiwan to Osaka. I was late for my flight and hurriedly handed my luggage, passport and shot certificates to the counter attendant. She rapidly pushed me through.

When I arrived in Osaka, the Osaka officials asked for my shot certificates again. In those days, shot certificates were required at both ends of a destination. If one failed to show the proper shot certificates, one might be fined and deported. I then realized that I carelessly had left one of my certificates on the counter in Taiwan.

Magically, six white-robed gentlemen appeared from

nowhere, pulled me aside, escorted me to a small office, laid me on a bench, inoculated me with boosters and handed me a new shot certificate. When I was reunited with my associates and tried to explain what happened, they turned deaf ears.

"Hans," they said, "We'll believe anything and don't even want to know."

A few days previously, we had sat in a small bar in Korea. Three attractive hostesses entertained us. I ordered a drink for myself and one for my lady companion. Then I tasted hers. Hers was water. I tasted it again. I was right the first time. Hers had no alcohol. Immediately I jumped up, ran over to the bartender and began to argue.

I was certain that the hostess had been cheated. It never occurred to me that I was the one who had been taken. Fortunately, one of my fellow buyers came to the rescue.

"Look, you idiot," he exclaimed, "if you were in Chicago, you would have a huge knife sticking in your ribs about now. Just leave the bartender alone." I followed his advice.

While in Hong Kong, I strolled down a dark and dismal-looking street. I attempted to locate a certain tea for my San Francisco grocer. He had emigrated from Hong Kong some years previously and had asked me to purchase this particular tea for him. I didn't realize that his variety came from Peking, whose products were off limits to all Americans at that time.

After going to a number of tea shops and wandering ever deeper into hidden alleys and back streets, I found the tea. Then I wrapped the tea in some fresh underwear and brought it back into the United States. It was either that or change my grocer.

Back home, my grocer stated that the tea proved much coarser than what he was able to purchase in San Francisco's Chinatown. This incidence also was the last time I risked life, limb and reputation for good will.

On the other hand, I had some wonderful adventures as well. Once, I savored an unforgettable experience in Osaka. The three of us and our interpreter were walking down a very congested street. Suddenly, a young lady walked up to us, asked if we came from the United States and blushed profusely.

We told her we were Americans while our interpreter shook his head and chastised her under his breath. No proper Japanese woman would ever initiate a conversation, he proclaimed. She had to be a street woman. We should drop her. At once.

But she seemed very pleasant and although her vocabulary was quite limited, we invited her for lunch. Our interpreter didn't like this at all, even though she ordered nothing. Instead, she asked us a variety of questions about the States. She told us that she loved America and always wanted to go there. And someday she would, she said.

At the end of lunch, she asked if she might show us around the following day, which was a Sunday. My friends declined, but I immediately accepted.

The next morning she picked me up at my hotel. We climbed into a cab, drove to the train station, took the bullet train to Kyoto and then a "milk" train to Nara. In Nara she gave me a brief tour. At the end, I invited her for lunch. During lunch, she excused herself and made a phone call.

Apparently her mother, a widow, lived nearby and had asked us for dinner. I accepted with pleasure. What would be more enjoyable than dining in a traditional Japanese home with traditional Japanese food? I was thrilled. The young lady's mother seemed charming and lived in a beautiful home overlooking the valley.

I sat in the guest of honor's seat and was served a remarkable variety of traditional Japanese fare. The mother kept on apologizing that she only had normal food and that she didn't have time to purchase special delicacies. I was ecstatic. What more could I have asked for than a normal meal? Apparently, there were four daughters in this family. Each specialized in a different skill. One in business, one in cooking, a third in teaching and my friend in music.

That evening, the cooking daughter was home and helped prepare the delicious meal. Afterwards, my friend entertained us on their piano. And at the very end, the two sisters took me by cab and train back to my hotel. I felt blessed. Throughout the day, I had experienced an unusually enjoyable and charitable aspect of Japanese culture, which very few Americans ever have the privilege of seeing for themselves.

The following day, I related my story to our interpreter, who claimed that in twenty years of interpreting, he never had heard of such an experience. I, on the other hand, took it as a slice of life. But I also realized that my little side adventure in Osaka may have been the silver lining of my trip.

Over a period of time, I developed a knack for idiosyncrasies. From my point of view, I only did what was right. If this behavior included a touch of the unconventional, I couldn't help it.

In San Francisco, our personnel manager and I once attended a very boring "success story" meeting in our board room. At this particular meeting, various managers related their achievements. Although some of these seemed innovative, most proved old hat.

When our turn came, we claimed that we agreed with most of what had been said, but had followed an old methodology. With that, our personnel manager spread a black velvet cloth on the table, and I placed an opaque crystal ball in its center. We received tumultuous applause.

In this same board room, on another occasion, I received an urgent telephone message. All messages were screened, and only those of sufficient importance got through. As soon as any message was brought in, nearby managers craned their necks in order to read it.

When I opened my note, I saw these words, "Your mother wants to know if you are coming home for dinner." My neighbors on all sides fell off their chairs with laughter, and I never understood how that particular message got through.

Another time, I attended a meeting of hundreds of executives. We all were crammed into a small auditorium, waiting to hear the chairman of the board give his annual state of the union address. He acknowledged that business appeared soft and encouraged us to turn the trend around. Later he opened the floor for suggestions.

I had been doodling. When he opened the floor I already had my answer.

"Why not," I suggested, "circulate a different sales slogan every day? In that manner, everyone can become involved and we can bring business back with vigor. Furthermore," I added, "if everyone here comes up with five slogans, we would have enough catchwords for the next decade. Here are mine."

"Yeah or nay, we're here to stay,"

"Bust or burst, the customer's first."

"Timbuctu and Macy's, too."

"TLC the new decree."

"Do what's right and win the fight."

After a moment of silence, I received a standing ovation. One newcomer turned to a friend of mine and disdainfully said, "

"Why, he wasn't listening to the chairman at all. He was doodling." Of course, he was right.

Over the course of time, I served under numerous presidents and CEOs. Once, one of them visited our store and mulled over various changes we might make. One of these possibilities suggested that we close our record department. He inquired how much business the record department brought in, and I responded eagerly.

"One hundred and eighty thousand dollars," I guessed.

"That much?" he asked incredulously.

I raced into my office to substantiate my figures. The real figure was approximately half of what I said. I quickly caught up with the chairman.

"When you inquired about the volume for records, did you mean how much business we made every year or every two years?" I asked.

"Every year, of course," he tartly replied.

"Well, annually," I stated with great authority, "we only do ninety thousand dollars. I thought you meant every two years."

He looked at me like I came from the moon, but as I had offered my answer with such conviction, he let me off the hook.

On another occasion, I was less fortunate. At the time I was the camera buyer, and our camera department made an unusually high profit. Far higher than any other division. Part of the reason stemmed from the way we accounted for our film processing, which followed a different accounting method than the other divisions.

One day, a senior merchant from one of these other divisions called and asked why we were so successful. I told him. He thanked me and asked me to drop him a note with the incidentals. I told him I would.

That afternoon, I mentioned my phone call to my supervisor. He forbade me to write such a letter. When I asked him why, he said because he had said so. When I asked him again, he proceeded to explain we might have to change our way of accounting to follow that of the other divisions. New accounting procedures meant less profit. Less profits meant smaller bonuses. Smaller bonuses meant no letter.

"But I promised," I dutifully explained.

"And I told you no letter," snarled my boss.

I pondered a little and then came up with a solution.

"Why not write a letter that says nothing," I suggested.

"Let me see it first," demanded my boss.

I wrote a two page letter which said very little. For me, this seemed an easy task in itself. My boss sanctioned the note and off it went.

Three years later, a new president was transferred to Macy's California. This was the same individual to whom I had sent my worthless epistle some years previously.

When I read the announcement, I gingerly went to my boss and whispered, "Say, when I wrote that letter, didn't I write it to this gentleman?"

"Yeah," my boss bemoaned, "I believe you did," and we both looked at each other dejectedly.

Fortunately, our new president never mentioned the letter.

That letter also taught me a new moral. Always expect the unexpected. In my life, that seemed easy. At the same time, I wondered why these peculiar events always occurred to me. Why me, I asked myself, why me?

Of course, unusual situations developed outside of work, too.

XIX

Mistaken Identity

ONCE, WHEN I WORKED IN SACRAMENTO, I STUCK both feet into my mouth so deeply that I almost choked on them. I had driven to San Francisco for a meeting, after which I planned to have dinner with an old friend, Carol. I had told her that I would call her in the afternoon.

My meeting ended much earlier than I anticipated, and I drove directly to her apartment. Her apartment sat near a park, and I decided to wait in the park. Every hour, I walked to the corner grocery store and phoned, to see if she had arrived. Finally, she answered.

"Hi Carol," I said kiddingly, "this is Tom." Of course, we both knew that I wasn't Tom, but I assumed that she recognized my voice.

"Hi Tom," she replied, "This is Sue," kidding me back. I felt her voice sounded strange, but didn't give it much thought.

"I just wanted to check on tonight's date," I continued.

"Of course we still have a date," she answered.

"Great. I finished work a little early and hoped you might be ready as well."

"I'm ready," she responded, "but Martha and Jack just dropped by, so why don't we have dinner here instead?"

I heard some laughter in the background, and although I didn't remember Martha or Jack, this slight change in plans certainly didn't seem unreasonable.

"What may I bring?" I volunteered.

"Why don't you bring some Chenin Blanc," she suggested.

"O.K., I will. One more thing." I added, "I haven't shaved. May I shave at your place?"

"Of course," she answered, and I heard some more giggling.

I purchased two bottles of Chenin Blanc and walked over to her apartment. In the hallway, I spread shaving cream liberally all over my face. I decided to enter with a big splash.

With two bottles of wine in one hand, a razor in the other and my face covered with shaving cream, I knocked on her door. After a few moments, she opened it, wringing wet and dressed in a bathrobe.

"What are you doing here so early?" she demanded in a shrill tone.

"What are you talking about? I just spoke to you," I defensively replied. "And where are Martha and Jack?"

It didn't take me too long to realize what had happened. I had misdialed her number and now found myself in a very awkward position. Carol refused to believe anything, and I was at a loss for words. While she showered, I spent the next half hour dialing similar numbers, trying to prove my point. I never found Sue again, and the evening, which had begun with so much promise, ended in a fizzle.

The only consolation that I received, which wasn't much, was that the unknown Tom would find himself in very deep water the next time he saw Sue. But that thought seemed poor compensation for an evening completely ruined by the mere fact that I had misdialed Carol's number in the first place.

Some months later, Carol got even, just by chance. I still worked in Macy's Sacramento when she invited me to a party. Apparently her aunt and uncle lived near Sacramento and were hosting a big get together. Her uncle was a cattle rancher and promised a delicious buffet, a pleasant crowd and good music. I accepted with pleasure.

Shortly after I arrived, I made two observations. The first was that I didn't know a soul, not that I had expected to. The second was that this was a family affair. Everyone seemed to be related, something I hadn't realized when Carol invited me.

Family affairs always make me nervous. Carol brushed my fears aside and assured me that everyone was just a friend.

"Don't worry," she said. "Just relax." And relax I did.

Later in the evening I found cause for alarm. I passed in front of a couch occupied by an elderly couple. They motioned me over and introduced themselves as an aunt and uncle. Then, in that unique tone of voice that make bachelors wince, they proclaimed,

"Oh Mr. Lehmann, how very nice to meet you. We have heard so many good things about you."

While they talked, they nodded eagerly and clasped my hands tightly. The very kind of clasp and knowing look that turn bachelor's legs into spaghetti.

Shortly afterwards, three of Carol's male cousins beckoned me over. These were not normal sized cousins, but rather Chicago Bears sized cousins. Each of them towered over me, and each of them appeared six sheets to the wind.

"Hey," one of them said, as he menacingly dug four salami-sized fingers into my midriff. "We've got a great idea. Why don't the three of us and you and Carol drive up to Reno tonight, and we'll get you hitched?"

I turned white as a sheet.

"You've got to be kidding," I immediately responded.

"You don't like Carol?" they growled and grew six inches in height.

"Of course I like her," I assured them. "But I think we should think this over."

"Naw," they replied. "She likes you. You like her. So we'll do it. Now."

And with that, they turned around to look for Carol.

I quickly ran and fortunately found Carol before they did. She felt the same way as I. Somehow, we managed to disappear and did so quickly.

For a few months afterwards, I didn't attend any kind of function, especially any kind where I didn't know a soul.

But time has a way of erasing memories. Some time later, I

had forgotten about that episode. I was on a short vacation in Los Angeles when I ran across a different kind of dilemma.

XX

Serendipity

INEVER FELT COMFORTABLE TALKING TO STRANGERS, particularly in bars. One evening this attitude changed. I was listening to Dixieland music in a Beverly Hills nightclub, when a man about my age walked in. He was escorting two female companions, one on each side. The more I observed, the more I became convinced that he really deserved no more than one companion, and I the other.

As I had little to lose, I began to form a plan. Slowly an idea unfolded. Rather than striking up a conversation with one of the ladies and probably being rebuked, why not attempt to talk to the young man. In fact, why not pretend to know him?

With some apprehension I walked towards the threesome and looked intently at the young man.

"Excuse me," I asked, not even glancing at his companions. "Weren't you in the Army in Europe?" At that time, most men our age had been in the service and many of them were stationed in Europe.

"No," he answered. I was in the Navy in the South Pacific."

"Well," I insisted, "perhaps you attended college in the Midwest?" I knew that many Californians had gone to universities throughout the United States, and possibly we had that in common.

"No," he answered, "I went to school in Southern California."

"Perhaps," I continued, you spent some time in San Francisco?" hoping that he had too.

"No," he grumbled, "I never ventured further north than San Louis Obispo," and turned away from me.

At this juncture I became very uncomfortable.

"You see," I fabricated, "I know you from somewhere, but just can't decide from where." I apologized and returned to my stool.

Just then he yelled, "Wait, where did you go to high school?"

"I went to a tiny school in Southern California," I replied. "You probably never heard of it," knowing all too well that most people had never discovered Webb.

"Where was it, and what was it called?"

"It was in Claremont," I answered, "and it was called Webb."

"That's where you know me from," he gleefully shouted. "I went there too."

I was stunned and must have shown my incredulity, but eagerly turned around and came back to his table. He was in the ninth grade when I was a senior, and now we discovered many things in common. In no time at all, we made up for lost years, and all I could do was refrain from shaking my head in disbelief. The evening ended up much better than it started and ended with all of us becoming friends.

Some people might have called this experience a coincidence. Others would have called it a happening. I called it serendipity. And it reminded me of another experience I encountered when I was a teenager.

I had made a pact with my father. I would only swim in the ocean when someone watched me, and only then, if I used a small life raft as well. In this manner, I could paddle to my heart's content.

One day I became bored and decided to watch the sunbathers from my raft. Now came the rub. I couldn't watch anyone without my glasses.

My father felt glasses were fine as long as they were worn on land. For glasses to be worn by a gawking teenager, in the ocean, was not his definition of common sense.

Somehow, I persuaded him that the waters seemed calm and that there was no need for concern. Eventually, being the kind father that he was, he agreed.

For half an hour I paddled up and down the beach, becoming increasingly enamored of the fine art of teenage gawking. Suddenly, a large breaker crashed down and threw me, my raft and my glasses in three different directions.

For once, I didn't need to see my father. I could feel the heat of his gentle soul begin to rise and quite rapidly at that. Meanwhile, the waves increased, and I barely managed to retrieve my raft.

With much determination, I swam toward shore. First I touched the bottom, and then I waded in. When I was up to my knees and about ten feet from my enraged father, I felt something under my feet. There were my glasses, not scratched and absolutely intact.

My father, of course, looked at my good fortune with very mixed emotions while I became ecstatic and floated on air.

I was reminded of similar good fortune some years later. I was on my way to Europe when I realized I had forgotten to acquire an international driver's license. I had one day left and raced to the AAA with my California driver's license, a passport photo and two dollars.

"Can't do it," the gentleman behind the counter informed me. "Your driver's license has expired." I panicked, raced to the DMV, scanned the written examination, barely passed and now needed to pass the actual driving test as well. Then I really became nervous.

It was raining. My car was a tiny VW, and the examiner who walked toward me demonstrated a distinct weather-worsened limp. His limp wouldn't improve in a miniature vehicle, and I began to cringe.

"What do you do?" he demanded.

I told him.

"Do you have any hobbies?"

I did.

"Who taught you to drive?"

I answered.

"I must apologize for these personal inquiries," he then explained, "but I never ask anyone their personal history unless they were born on the same day I was."

And at that moment I knew I was saved. And I was. Was that providence? Destiny? And how did these situations occur? Were they coincidences or luck? Or perhaps my fairy godmother was responsible? In any event, I felt that here was another case of pure serendipity. And, perhaps, a precursor of events to come.

XXI

The Facts Of Life Aren't Free

FOR ME, GOOD FORTUNE HAS ALWAYS SEEMED omnipresent. Even under peculiar circumstances. For instance, some years later, I encountered two bizarre events, both ending in a most unexpected fashion.

The first took place at Nepenthe, Big Sur's legendary restaurant. In those days Nepenthe opened on April Fool's Day and closed with a traditional masked ball on All Hallow's night.

Expected guests included Henry Miller, Eric "Party Pad" Nord and Jack Kerouac, and the local denizens spent months perfecting elaborate costumes for their mammoth social event.

I persuaded a friend to dye for me a pair of long johns, purple. Nowadays, you can buy all kinds of long johns, some even striped and weather proofed for skiing, but in those days not so.

I remember thinking what an ideal spot Nepenthe would be to go to. Perched at the edge of the rugged coast, it seemed one of the enchanting spots of the world. Warm, tranquil and rustic

On the designated night, I manipulated my ancient Dodge around the numerous curves and reached Nepenthe after 9:00 P.M. The clear night proved magical, with a warm wind and a tingling spell in the air. I saw costumes galore, elaborate hats, imposing masks and sparkling sequins.

Then I entered into a marvelous combination of the real, the surrealistic, Fasching in Mainz and a Paris arts ball. I jumped in with fervor, breathed the air of total abandonment and became engrossed with the wild spirits around me.

Shortly after I arrived, a lovely harem lady slithered close, looked me in the eyes and purred, "I like your lips."

I felt weak. No one had ever spoken to me like this. I had noticed her on entering, but also knew she was not alone. Perhaps this feeling of security enabled her to poach on unsuspecting men, or so I thought. With a skimpy dress and a low voice, she mockingly swayed with every word. She also indicated her friend seemed very possessive and that was that. "Too bad," she murmured, "too bad."

After our brief encounter, we drifted apart, but the entire night I continued to run into her. First inside, then outside and finally near the bar. The wind, the music and the laughter affected everyone, and I felt enraptured.

One last time I ran into, just her as she was leaving.

"We are staying at the Hot Springs," she whispered. "Why don't you come?"

With this brief statement she disappeared. But she also had left me bewildered. Was she a dream? Was she real? Should I go? Why not? Why yes? And where at the Hot Springs?

By the time I had collected my thoughts, it was 2:00 A.M. I decided to follow her and began the long and winding descent to Slate's Hot Springs. Today it is called Esalen, and it has become a well-known retreat.

In those days, the Springs included a primitive lodge, a bar and a few weathered bungalows. I saw a parking area and a few lights. That seemed the extent of the facilities.

A number of diehards sat at the bar. Some seemed stragglers. Others I recognized from Nepenthe, still in their costumes. No one cared about my arrival, and that seemed fine. My friend was nowhere in sight. What had I expected?

I ordered a drink and slowly realized that my femme fatale would never show. No matter, the night was a dream anyway.

"Too bad," she had said. Well, too bad.

After a long wait, I finally stood up to leave. As I turned, she suddenly appeared. Just like that. From out of nowhere she came, first apologizing for being late and then murmuring something about "him not having fallen asleep."

Quietly, she took me by the hand and led me out. She seemed to know exactly where to go.

"Let's go to the baths," she whispered. "There's no one there."

I had visited the natural mineral baths a couple of times previously and knew that the path was steep. But the stars shone, the night was idyllic and after all, why not? The steep and rocky trail ended in a fork. Women descended to the left and men to the right. A few knotty boards surrounded each area and an old rickety fence separated the actual baths.

The baths sat on a narrow ledge, one hundred fifty feet above the roaring surf. Four tubs were embedded in the sandy soil, each with a spigot of hot mineral water. Cold water came from a nearby faucet, and one mixed one's own bath. The old wooden railings stuck out dangerously.

We both walked to the right, and I remember thinking myself in a dream. The night was warm, the sky clear and the air sultry.

I looked around. My friend drew the water. Everything was silent, except for the violent surf below. I saw the crystal white spray of the breakers, pounding on the rocks beneath us.

The seven or eight foot ledge on which we found ourselves sat directly under the cliffs. A ponderous granite obtrusion, probably forty feet high, hung over our heads. This rock surrounded the ledge and, except for the weathered railings and narrow entrance, gave us the privacy of a hidden cloister.

I lowered myself into the tub slowly. The mirage continued, and there we lingered, hypnotized by the night, the air and each other.

Suddenly she stiffened, and I, like her twin, also froze.

"There's a light," she gasped. "There's a light and it's headed this way."

I turned around and easily made out the small light that wove down the path towards us. We did not move. Bewildered? Mesmerized? Unsure? Perhaps, we hoped the light might wander in another direction. Or turn back.

By the time we fully realized our predicament, time had run

out. I jumped up and tried to put on my clothing. Pulling on a pair of long johns at any hour is difficult. Getting into them at night, when one is wet and in a hurry, is virtually impossible. I jammed one leg down and tore off a piece of the arm.

Then the light blinded me. First the beam shone on me and then on my friend. I heard a voice. A growl.

"Mister," the voice snarled. I froze.

"Mister," only this time more slowly, more articulate. I shook like a leaf.

"Mister," once again and this time with a definite finality, and I remembered what she had said, "He is very possessive."

My alternatives seemed limited. A cliff impossible to scale. Four tubs to jump behind. A weather-beaten railing to hurdle over, only to fall straight down into the rolling surf below.

"Mister." This was it. I hardly breathed and barely heard the snarl.

"This lady is a guest. Visitors pay seventy-five cents."

It was the manager.

I quickly found seventy-five cents and gave it to him. Shortly thereafter, however, I beat a hasty retreat. No sense in pushing my luck too far, I decided, especially as my skin wasn't that tough to begin with. Did I have luck? Or good fortune? Or did my fairy godmother come to the rescue once again? In any event, I felt very, very fortunate.

XXII

Never Talk To Strangers

SOME TIME LATER, I INCURRED A SIMILAR PREDICA-
ment, also near the Pacific Ocean. A friend of mine and I
decided to go camping in the picturesque town of Mendocino.
Much to our dismay, every camping spot seemed booked. The
more we looked, the more we realized we would not find a vacant
site. We elected to camp without a site.

The spot we chose proved well hidden and rather isolated.
We needed to be secluded as we had decided to camp in a nature
preserve. We knew nature preserves weren't intended for camping, and we planned to be especially careful with the environment.

We camped above a small cove at the edge of the water. Early
in the morning, I awoke to the sound of gun shots over our heads.
Initially, I thought I had imagined the noise but then knew differ-
ently. I heard the distinct sound of bullets whining from above. I
also knew that the bullets flew far too close for comfort.

My friend, who slept more soundly than I, also wakened.

"What was that?" she inquired.

"I'm not sure, but I believe it was a gun." And we remained
very still.

Then the shooting began again, and I realized that some kids
probably were taking pot shots into the surf. They didn't realize
we were camped beneath them, and they were enjoying their
"Sunday fun."

"Hey," I yelled.

The shots stopped, but then began again.

"Hey, there's someone down here," I shouted, even louder than before.

The shots stopped but then began once more.

Then peace, followed by two more shots.

"Hey, don't you know it's Sunday?" my friend suddenly yelled.

"We're not religious," came the reply.

"Neither am I," she screamed back. "I'm trying to sleep."

Stillness and then another shot.

"Hans, please tell them to shut up," my friend pleaded.

Surely I lacked many qualities, especially those of John Wayne. But with my ego on the line, and possibly my life as well, I knew I needed to go. After all, what harm could come from a couple of teenagers?

I slowly pulled on my jeans, reached for my boots and rambled off. I recently had begun a course in judo and naively felt somewhat confident. The trail proved well hidden. Neither the noisy intruders nor I could see each other until I confronted them directly.

At that point I choked. Rather than two, there were six. And instead of teenagers, they had become grown ups. Four men and two women, wide awake, ominous and very suspicious as to who their Lone Ranger might be.

One of the men, the tallest, was slapping a small pistol from hand to hand.

"Yeah, man, what's up?" he inquired as his muscles flexed in the morning light.

"Not much," I ventured, trying to hide my shaking knees. "But don't pay any attention to that broad, she doesn't know what she's talking about." I decided that the term "broad" seemed as appropriate as any word at that particular moment. Then I suggested further.

"Look, we really don't care if you shoot or not, but you know this is a nature preserve. If you get picked up, so do we. That's all."

"And," I added, as my adrenalin and creative juices began to flow, "I don't know if you know it, but there's a Highway Patrolman's convention here this weekend. I've never seen so many patrol cars in my life."

It was true I had seen a couple of patrol cars, and I felt it didn't hurt to magnify this observation.

"You're kidding," the tall one exclaimed.

"Just try me," I calmly answered, casually shrugging my shoulders. At the same time, I became very conscious that the pistol took on the size of a cannon.

"Well thanks, man."

"No sweat," I answered, as I slowly turned back and tried to hide the rivers of perspiration that began to cascade down my face.

The minute I left their sight, I hurtled towards our camping spot, grabbed my friend, sleeping bags and all, and ran towards the car. Then I dumped my squirming armload inside and careened off.

"What was all that about?" my friend asked incredulously."

"You'll never believe it," I gasped. And I almost didn't either.

Since then, I have visited Mendocino many times. I even have camped there on occasion. But I never camped without a reservation again. No sense in provoking lightning twice, or so I decided.

I also decided that it was time to enlarge my list of social acquaintances. Too many times I seemed to be soliciting danger with the friends that I had. Perhaps it was time for me to expand my social horizons. And I pondered various alternatives.

XXIII

Witty, Attractive And Wise

UNEXPECTEDLY, A COUSIN SENT ME SIX PAGES OF personal classified from the *New York Magazine*, not to be confused with *The New Yorker*. To me, these pages seemed enlightening. I always considered dating a personal affair. Yet here I scanned a popular magazine that not only listed wines, restaurants and reviews, but hosted numerous personal ads as well.

These began as follows: "Megawatt Green Eyes," or "Refined but Earthy," or "Extremely Attractive and Charming, 37, seeks successful single man, 40 plus, who responds to a winning smile and a warm wit. Send biography and photo."

Nor were these personals cheap, even if they did reach a million readers. At twenty-seven dollars a line, the average advertisement (which included a New Jersey box number) probably cost two hundred and fifty dollars.

Who wrote these? Who answered them? What were the results? The more I wondered, the more interested I became.

Never having been married, I had nothing to lose, or so I decided, and answered a few personals that sounded especially appealing. The more I answered, the more confused I became. One day I made the ultimate decision. I would write my own ad instead. Three thousand miles seemed a good buffer, or so I believed.

After countless hours of writing, rewriting and editing, I wrote as follows:

California bachelor (Monterey) reasonably cultured, secure and
spontaneous, seeks female companion, witty, attractive and wise.
Must be an energetic, sportive and unpretentious non-smoking
diurnal, who enjoys classical music, art and the great outdoors.

I wasn't going to leave anything to chance.

I had no idea what to expect. Why should I? On the other hand, I felt that if I received a dozen or so answers, I would be satisfied. I decided that if there were three or four hundred advertisements, mostly written by easterners for easterners, why should anyone even recognize a lowly Californian?

How mistaken I was!

Within two weeks after my ad ran, I received a hefty envelope from *New York Magazine*. In it I found some twelve letters. The next day I received seven. Then five. And so on. Within three weeks, I had received over forty responses. Long letters, short letters, vague letters, specific letters, some with photographs and some without, but mostly very, very personal.

Included were some Xeroxed letters and some advertisements. For the most part, however, every respondent indicated a sincere interest in writing me. I was floored. Here I knew numerous friends who rarely wrote and then only in platitudes. Now suddenly quite a few sincere, presumably witty and unknown individuals were offering to befriend me.

But trouble was beginning. One lady wrote, enclosing a photograph, address, age and phone number, and proclaimed all possible virtues and interests for, not herself, but her daughter.

Another lady answered my ad, after a well-meaning friend sent it to her. A third unwittingly turned out to be acquainted with my secretary. I received answers from New York, New Jersey, Connecticut, California, Texas and Vermont.

Certainly I didn't want to offend anyone. On the other hand, how could I start any kind of relationship, even a pen club, with over forty individuals? One lady wrote, "I am sure that by this time, you have had many responses and are trying to figure out which one to start with." How right she was.

Another wrote, "I am a unique woman for all seasons. If you

are truly interested in enjoying the best things in life, please send a photo and letter to me." I didn't feel inclined. Not that I minded, but if I didn't ask for a photo, why should she? Also, I felt that she would have preferred a bank statement as well.

I began this venture shortly before Macy's hectic holiday season and consequently did not find much spare time. I also didn't know what one did with forty aspiring friends.

After great deliberation, I decided that my only solution would be to develop a questionnaire. Not a normal questionnaire, but a very private one that touched on specific issues I liked and didn't like. That way, I might get some idea of the desires and interests of my new-found acquaintances.

After a week, I concocted three pages of simple multiple choice questions. These asked the respondents to rank their preferences in order of one to three.

I allowed room for optional comments and added, "if you like all three choices equally, you may write three 'ones,' or if you vehemently dislike all three, write in three 'threes." In short, a seemingly easy choice for anyone to decipher and for me to interpret. With hardly a backward glance, I sent them out, not to everyone who answered, but to about a third. I felt fifteen correspondents were plenty.

Then I answered the questionnaire myself, ranked the questions, and made comments of my own. In this way, I could compare their answers to mine and also add or subtract points for questions especially important to me.

For instance, some typical questions were: "Would you prefer a baseball game, a football game or a bull fight? (I liked football.) Or "would you prefer a Bed and Breakfast, a five star hotel or staying with friends?" I enjoyed staying with friends and loathed five star hotels. Most respondents preferred the hotels. "Would you prefer to cook for six, cook for two or dine out?" This answer might have suggested their culinary abilities.

The answers ranged all over the map and the comments seemed even more surprising. One lady wrote, "What the questionnaire fails to take into account, is the difference between things that one actually likes to do for having done them, and those that one thinks one would like to do because one knows nothing about them." Very true.

Another answered, "Sorry about all the crisscrosses and white-outs, but my sister and brother-in-law wanted to answer them, too."

A third wrote, "I find multiple choice questions inhibit creativity, so I wrote a letter instead." Comparing a philosophy to a family answer to a detailed letter was not exactly an easy task. But I was game, as long as my new-found friends were, and so, one by one, I replied to their answers. Most respondents asked additional questions, and I asked more from them.

Most wanted to know why a Californian placed an ad in a New York magazine. I was beginning to wonder the same. One lady wrote, "Have you already exhausted all the best women on the West Coast, or are you so notorious for your evil ways that no California girl will go out with you? I'm suspicious, but interested." So was I.

Another wrote, "Are you looking for a pen pal or are there enough ladies in California who read *New York Magazine* to make it worth your while?" Still, a fourth wrote, "I thought your ad the most refreshing one I've read and am curious to find out more about you." (And me about her.) A fifth asked if I was a "shrink." And on it went.

Every evening, I scurried home from work in order to check my mail. My nights became restless, meals suffered, shadows formed under my eyes, and although every day began with a smile, my real thoughts were: "What will the mail bring next?" or more importantly, "What have I gotten myself into this time?"

My files burgeoned five inches thick and although my phone remained silent, I knew this intrusion might be next. Perhaps even a trip to New York City. Now I really began to worry. My budget barely allowed one ad, let alone long distance phone calls and surely not cross-country jaunts.

After the second or third round of correspondence, certain patterns began to emerge. Small nuances appeared, likes and dislikes developed, ideological differences became apparent. Before long, my list of fifteen prospects had dwindled to five.

These five established a very potent force. Letters that had been signed "sincerely" and "regards," changed to "affectionately" and "love." I became nervous and still didn't know one person from another.

I decided to fly to Manhattan. Surely these new-found friends were not the only reason, but probably the prime reason. In addition, discretion suggested I initiate a more thorough investigation than that pursued by mere correspondence. Budgets could be forgotten once in a while.

Some weeks later, I arrived in the Big Apple. I had assured my five correspondents that we definitely would get together. But I was naive. Of my five friends, one was out of town. A second had fallen in love with someone else. A third no longer seemed interested in pursuing a three thousand mile courtship, not that I blamed her.

Of the other two femmes fatales, we had pleasant times together. Both seemed amenable, attractive, witty and wise. But I was reminded of Rudyard Kipling. Mr. Kipling wrote, "East is East and West is West and never the twain shall meet, 'till earth and sky stand presently at God's great judgment seat."

Somehow, Manhattan didn't appear to be the proper judgment seat. Or maybe I was intimidated. In any event, shortly after I arrived in New York City, I turned my direction homeward again. Nor have I placed any more personal ads. One unexpected Manhattan journey seemed enough. I decided to limit my social engagements to the West Coast.

XXIV

Bachelor Number Two

IDECIDED TO TRY OUT FOR THE ORIGINAL "DATING Game," a West Coast television show. In this way, I could remain in the West and still pursue my social activities. I always had enjoyed this show, in which three bachelors were interviewed by a supposedly winsome bachelorette. Part of the intrigue seemed to be that neither party saw the other.

The bachelorette asked each bachelor a number of mundane questions.

"Bachelor Number One," she inquired, "what is your favorite movie? Do you prefer dogs or cats? If we had a date, where would you take me?" And so on.

Depending on their responses, she then decided which bachelor she wished to date. Finally, with considerable fanfare, the master of ceremonies introduced these two "blind dates," and offered them marvelous prizes. These prizes generally meant a vacation to the Bahamas, a skiing sojourn in Aspen, a week's cruise on "The Love Boat," or a similar treasure.

To me, playing a game of this magnitude seemed the ultimate prize, and so I applied to get on the show. Two weeks later, I received an answer, advising me where to go and when.

On the appointed day, I drove to Los Angeles and found the proper street. I assumed it would be a wide boulevard with a bright new office building. Rather, it seemed a dismal street, surrounded by dilapidated structures. Obviously a camouflage, in order to keep the hordes of other prospective bachelors at bay.

Much to my dismay, three or four hundred prospects stood in line, eagerly awaiting their turn.

I discovered that this show interviewed bachelors and bachelorettes by the score. Bachelors on the even days. Bachelorettes on the odd. Being a candidate proved nothing. There literally were thousands a week. One needed to be a winner here, in order to be selected for the show.

I waited in line for two hours, along with everyone else. Most of my fellow prospects appeared to be unemployed actors. Almost all had agents. None came from Northern California, and each felt he would win. So did I.

I was reminded of my first day in the Army. Too many candidates. Too many rooms. Far too many bad jokes and an endless amount of waiting.

Eventually I found myself in front of a desk where a young lady, who chewed at least six sticks of gum, mechanically handed me an application blank, clipboard and pen. Then I waited some more. At one point, someone took my Polaroid photo. On occasion, a representative led us into yet another room, and then we waited again. I began feeling like a cow ready for slaughter. In this manner, the morning progressed.

Finally, we sensed a certain electricity in the air. We knew that our time had arrived. Every few minutes an assistant called out three names, and three eager souls clutched their coats, application blanks and Polaroid photos and walked optimistically through a wooden door. None emerged again.

Then someone called my name, and I followed two other bachelors who walked ahead of me. These two were my immediate competition, or so I assumed. I was right.

Shortly thereafter, we found ourselves in a sparsely furnished room. Here another aid told us to sit on a bench. To our right sat three other candidates who were going to try their luck first. In front of us waited two stern-faced gentlemen who looked like university professors preparing to hear an oral exam. Reams of books and legal pads surrounded them. Presumably, they were our judges.

I felt very nervous. My mind proceeded at fast forward. I also watched the other group of bachelors answer an array of questions, fired at them by their unseen bachelorette.

Their answers proved mediocre at best. Almost anyone might have responded better than they did, or so I thought. Finally, one of the "professors" dismissed them with a curt "thank you" and sent them on their way. Our turn came next, and I began to feel even more queasy than before.

Our unseen examiner asked my two competitors some questions, none of which I can recall. I do know their answers seemed trite. My mind continued to run out of control. Between the long wait, the self-made pressures and high expectations, my entire system began to run on a very automatic pilot.

I was "Bachelor Number Two," and felt unusually tense. Finally the bachelorette spoke to me. Our dialogue went as follows:

"Bachelor Number Two, how much money do you have in your pockets?"

"Ten dollars, nineteen and one half cents." (Don't ask me why I said half a cent. Somehow, it blurted out.)

"Bachelor Number Two, name the seven ways of signifying you are dead." (I believe she really said, "Name the seven deadly sins," but when your mind is out of control, what can you do?) I answered,

"You can't breathe. You can't see. You can't smell. And you become drowned by the tears of your loved ones." At this point, my mind blanked out again and then I added, "And the next three are a repeat of the first four."

"Bachelor Number Two, what is your favorite noise?" Fortunately, I managed to over-ride my automatic pilot and let out a shrill yodel. No one, but no one, had ever yodeled in that room before. Surely, I must have received some extra points, or so I hoped.

"Bachelor Number Two, if you and I went out for dinner tonight, what would we do?"

"Well, first I would trade in my half cent for thirty cents, as that is its true worth. (I was stalling for time.) "Then I would buy a bottle of wine and some bread and cook you a spaghetti dinner.

"And then?" she inquired impishly.

"And then," I said, as my mind went into a complete tailspin and my years in retailing took their toll, "I would charge you only fifty cents."

"You would what?" she shrieked in disbelief, (and the words TILT, TILT, TILT raced across my mind.)

Moments later, we also discovered ourselves summarily dismissed. Apparently the judges felt that bachelorettes should not be charged for their dinners.

Outside in the corridor, we congratulated each other and briefly compared notes. My companions thought I performed the best. Their laud seemed small consolation for finding myself on the street once again. Nor did I ever hear from "The Dating Game." Not that I expected to. Instead, I drove back up the coast, believing that my downfall had been the fifty-cent dinner. And then I realized that paying for dinners always had seemed to be one of my weaknesses. Even before "The Dating Game," dinner checks always seemed a problem.

XXV

Eating At Home Is Simpler

IONCE SPENT A FEW DAYS AT LAKE TAHOE AND MET A woman who was vacationing with her parents. This woman asked if I would like to join her and her parents for a dinner show at Harrah's. I accepted with pleasure. I also assumed that her father, who seemed to be a very successful San Francisco attorney, would foot the bill.

That evening, the four of us drove to the casino. When we arrived, sixteen friends of theirs waited to join us. Soon all twenty of us sat at one long table. The dinner was good, the show excellent. And I enjoyed myself thoroughly.

After the show, we all sat around while the waitress brought the checks. She began with the couple across from me, who paid for themselves. Then the next couple, who did likewise. Then the third couple and so forth. In this fashion, the waitress walked around the entire table, collecting money.

Meanwhile, I glanced at my date and at her father. I also made a great pretense at hunting for my wallet. I felt that if he was going to pay, he would have said something at that point. But he said nothing, and I couldn't believe he hadn't noticed my wild wallet-seeking gyrations.

Instead, none of the family showed any concern whatsoever. Rather, they continued to carry on a lively and animated conversation with everyone at the table.

Finally the waitress stood at my elbow, and after looking at the father one more time, I begrudgingly paid for both my date and myself. Then the waitress came to the father, who casually pointed in my direction and stated that he would pay for the four of us. The waitress explained that I already had paid. The father looked at me disdainfully, apologized and offered to reimburse me. Common sense should have prevailed, but I declined. A sense of meaningless pride had taken over.

The father, somewhat nonplused, insisted we go to another nightclub, where he would pay. In this manner, he proved his original intent. By the time we returned home, at a very early hour in the morning, the entire evening had left a very bitter taste in my mouth. I also realized that when it came to paying for almost anything, I really lacked class. When it came to paying for dinners, especially, I should have my head examined.

Some years later, I was offered another free meal, but under totally different circumstances Once again I turned it down, presumably because of too much pride.

I had skied in Taos, New Mexico, and was returning home. Another skier suggested that if I went through Santa Fe, I had to stay at the La Fonda Hotel and must stop at a certain restaurant. He told me that I shouldn't miss either one. I followed his advice, stayed at the La Fonda and made dinner reservations. Somehow, I assumed that the restaurant was a modest Mexican restaurant. Instead, I discovered a very elegant French establishment, first class in every respect, especially the price. I wore my ski clothes and felt awkward, but was seated.

When the waiter came, he asked if I cared for a cocktail. I told him I preferred wine with dinner. He nodded agreement and left. For an eternity I sat alone, without anyone coming to my table again.

Meanwhile, my waiter served appetizers to other guests who arrived after I did. I became increasingly frustrated, got up, asked for my coat and walked out. I decided that the restaurant really didn't need me any more than I needed it.

Suddenly, at my side, appeared the maitre d'.

"Excuse me, sir," he said in a pronounced French accent, "but what happened?"

"Nothing," I replied. "Exactly nothing. I sat there. No one came. And I left."

"But that is impossible, sir, please accept my apologies. Please come back."

"No," I said, as I walked out the front door. "But thank you very much."

"Please, sir, we are trying to make this the finest restaurant in the South West. Please come back. I implore you."

By now we stood outside.

"Look," I said, "I realize I should have worn a tie, and next time I will. And I can understand your position, but I am leaving."

"Sir, you are mistaken. Your clothing is fine. There is nothing wrong with it. Please come back. Please come back, or you will ruin my weekend."

By now we had walked half way across the parking lot, and I felt somewhat foolish.

"Look," I finally said. "Someday I will return, I assure you, but I will wear a tie when I do."

"Sir," he replied. "Once again, I implore you. There is nothing the matter with your attire." And then he added, "Would it make any difference if you came back as my guest?"

That offer stumped me. Having been taught the importance of good customer service throughout much of my life, I nevertheless thought that this suggestion went beyond the call of duty."

"I will come back," I answered, "but let me pay."

"As you wish, sir," he responded, "but then let me take care of the wine."

"Fine," I answered, and back we went.

When I entered this time, I received the best table. Rolls and butter rained upon me like water. I felt like a king and was handled as such, and ended up by consuming a superb meal.

Towards the end of my dinner, I overheard the maitre d' offer some of his vintage port to a nearby table. Noticing me, he instructed his waiter, "And to this gentleman, too,"

In this manner, the meal ended up much better than it had started. In fact, it was superb.

At the same time, the entire evening confirmed what I always suspected. Eating out seemed a nuisance. One must decide where to eat. What to order. And who will pay. Given the choice, I will take a home-cooked meal over a restaurant, any day, any time and anywhere. Regardless who pays.

On the other hand, when it came to hospitality, the restaurant certainly had it. At the end, I was shown such excellent service, that I almost couldn't believe my eyes. If only I might instill the same service at Macy's. But I was unable to do so. And after twenty-eight years in retailing, I decided to retire. I decided that I wanted to search for fresh waters in which to sail. One day I informed my boss that I planned to take early retirement. I told him I wanted to seek new endeavors. In fact, I told him I wanted to become an inventor.

XXVI

A Dog Of A Dish

I ALWAYS DREAMT OF BECOMING FAMOUS. AND RICH. But lying dormant was the strongest urge of all, to become a rich and famous inventor. To be thrown into the same stratosphere as that of Leonardo da Vinci, Benjamin Franklin and Thomas Edison. To nibble at my glasses and gaze wistfully into the sky while dozens of eager associates begged for my attention. No doubt about it, I would become an inventor.

I began to plot and plan. Ideas shot through my head night and day. Simple ideas, fancy ideas, complicated ones and trifling ones, all sorts of grandiose schemes that would transfer me into instant success. But where should I start? Where should I begin?

One evening, while dining with friends and vigorously pursuing my now compulsive dream, I heard them ask:

"What about Jim? Do you know Jim? Why not him?"

Apparently Jim was a good friend of theirs and a patent attorney of the first rank. Smart, honest and very able. He had challenged the industrial giants of the world and beaten them handily. Obviously, my type of attorney.

Some time later, I made an appointment. I tried to disregard his immaculate desk, walnut walls and glass-enclosed conference room. I wanted to think of him as just another guy, who wanted to help another person in need.

Jim acted as nobody's fool. For an hour he grilled me, asked me if I really knew what I was attempting and clearly identified the problems, the costs, the risks. With each barrier, I became more convinced than ever that the end of the rainbow seemed near. Obstacles or not, I felt compelled to go ahead.

When Jim ultimately acquiesced, I suggested various possibilities. Some proved unpatentable, others unwise or unrealistic. One, however, harbored those particular characteristics inherent in future fame. One seemed a winner for sure, my spill-proof dog dish. Not completely spill-proof, mind you, but certainly perfect for the traveler or normal dog lover. Indeed, a very profound item.

Jim agreed to conduct a patent search, and I planned to create a few samples. More than six months later and hundreds of dollars poorer, I still was developing my first model. I discovered that most dog dishes were made from plastic. They were produced by either an extrusion process or a vacuum process. The extrusion process seemed far more efficient, but necessitated an initial outlay of $30,000. A vacuum process only required a few hundred dollars for a mold, but upped the per-unit manufacturing cost of each dish four fold. As I didn't have $30,000, I decided on the vacuum process.

My source of all this worldly information came from a plastic genius named Jerry. He came recommended to me by that circuitous but age-old route known as the yellow pages. Like Jim, Jerry thought me somewhat daffy, but he too seemed willing to try.

Some time later, after making numerous marketing studies, preliminary drawings and clay prototypes, I finally owned my first wooden mold. A small firm which specialized in wooden molds made it.

This firm also specialized in reaping high profits for itself, and within a short period of time I paid for three different versions, each slightly different than its predecessors and each more expensive. Visualizing the perfect mold proved as difficult for me, as it was for the firm to produce. Nevertheless, through trial and error, we finally developed the perfect sample.

By now, my ledger bulged with numerous entries, all debits, and all expensive:

ledger
patent attorney
patent search
drafting charges
wooden molds
set up charges
production costs
checking account
rubber stamps (for the sales slips)
business license
shipping cartons
wrapping tape
address labels
sales slips

I also rented a private mail order box for business purposes. I felt I was in business, or at least ready, and therefore only needed to decide how many bowls I wanted to produce on my first run. Jerry and I devoted countless hours mulling over the perfect quantity. We finally decided to produce only a minimal number at first, until the sales rolled in. We also replaced the wooden molds with leaden ones.

Though these leaden molds added considerably to the cost, they were far more durable than the wooden ones. They also enabled us to be ready for the inevitable sales explosion.

Finally, I debated the proper method of advertising. How should I advertise and where should I advertise and how much should I charge for the end product? Certainly, the most finite of all retailing questions.

I decided to consult the oldest textbook in the world, namely the seat of my pants. I felt that a mail-back coupon in *Sunset Magazine* seemed the only way to go. Fast, reliable and efficient, and a method from which I would reap all the profits. No middle man for me, just the raw dollars, or so I hoped.

My next step necessitated producing a photo for the ad. Fortunately, my dog loved every minute. In no time, he had posed for over twenty shots. Close up shots, far away shots, slurping shots and licking shots. You name them, we had them.

The best of these photos I sent to *Sunset Magazine*, with a rough layout. A few months later, the proof came back and with it some more bills. But the proof impressed me, and I O.K.'d the ad. Now I only had to wait for the actual magazine to appear.

Finally, the actual magazine issue came out, and I raced down to the news stand. What a day! What an ad! Perfect placement. Beautiful reproduction. Excellent copy. (After all, I wrote it.) And all the other necessities of a first class advertisement.

The ad stated: "Safe, sound and virtually spill proof. High outside rim resists splashing; shallow inside moat deters insects; deep concave well retains fluids; perfect for travel or home."

What happened then remains a mystery. Although I received plenty of responses, they were either from advertising agencies, soliciting my business, or from gardeners hoping to sell me another product. Perhaps my bowl proved too expensive, no one needed it or a host of other possibilities.

Suffice it to say, and much to my dismay, the response from the ad barely paid for the address labels, let alone for the ad and certainly not for the bowls, which piled up high in my garage.

Shortly thereafter, I received a note from my attorney with a letter from the patent office. It seemed that my original patent application needed further clarification, and the patent office sent me sketches of various patents, including those of a cat dish, a chick feeder and a safety holder for burning sulfur. All of these held sway over my patent request. Did I, asked Jim, wish to pursue my quest further?

After long deliberation, I reluctantly said no. I now was over five thousand dollars in the hole and didn't relish the thought of digging any deeper. In addition, who said I needed to be an inventor anyway? It was merely a whim.

Two days later I read about an Ohio farmer who had cornered the earthworm market. That profession was something I really could sink my teeth into. Surely, inventors were a dime a dozen and seemed no big deal, but earthworm farmers represented a horse of a different color and served a useful purpose as well. I would become a farmer, that's what. But after much thought, I decided that earthworms weren't my cup of tea either. In fact, I suddenly realized that I wasn't sure what I wanted to do.

And then it dawned on me. I might do anything. I was retired. Free as a bird. I might travel, write, garden, hike, walk my dog, help non-profits, host house guests, ring the Salvation Army bell, put myself up for bid at charity bachelor auctions, become a jail-bird for charity and on. The list proved endless. My only concern was the fact that I probably would run out of money. And soon. With this thought in mind, I thought of additional projects that would bring in some income. I might hire myself out as Santa, dog sit, rent out my house and so forth.

I decided to try all of these possibilities, profit and non-profit alike. I also was under the illusion that nothing could go wrong. How little I knew!

XXVII

Winnings Aren't For Losers

SHORTLY BEFORE I RETIRED, I HAD WON A TRIP TO LAS Vegas, courtesy of a ten dollar raffle ticket. After I retired, I decided to use it. The trip included everything except transportation, and so I made reservations, hopped into my car and drove off. With a paid vacation, I was home free, or so I assumed.

I spent the first night in Bakersfield, at a restaurant and motel combination. If you ever visited Bakersfield and didn't stay in town, you missed a lot. Where else could you find a reasonable room, an inexpensive meal and a live band to boot? Even my window blinds, which came tumbling down, didn't dampen my spirits. Who needed blinds to sleep with anyway?

The next day I left early and arrived at Las Vegas shortly before noon. Las Vegas offered much, but easy maneuverability wasn't one of its strengths. Every tourist followed the same route and literally thousands of cars, trucks, busses and motorcycles crawled up and down the main drag. On all sides I saw neon signs, high-rise buildings, gawking tourists, cement jungles and a host of energetic activity.

All the hotels looked impressive. Eventually I found mine, parked my car and strode into the lobby. My watch showed 1:00 P.M., and all I needed was a shower, a shave and a nap.

Unfortunately, a few hundred other guests arrived at the same time. The massive check-in counter resembled Kennedy Airport on Christmas Eve. Queues formed in front of every receptionist.

When I finally reached the front desk, the desk clerk informed me that my room wasn't ready.

"Maybe in about an hour," he said. "Maybe then."

An hour later my room still wasn't ready, nor two hours later. At 4:00 P.M. I intercepted the assistant manager and told him that if I didn't obtain a room at once, I would sleep on the floor.

"Mister," he bluntly declared, "I don't care where you sleep." So much for customer service. His reply foreshadowed an ominous beginning.

I knew my room number, hunted down my chamber maid and begged her to make up my room. With the aid of a deserved gratuity, she quickly cleaned my room, and by 5:00 P.M. I took my nap.

Actually, my room almost seemed worth the wait. A miniature football field for a bed, a radio console for a telephone and a panoramic view. Very nice and perfectly proper.

My prize allowed me almost anything. Later I discovered it didn't include my sauna nor the tiny bottle of suntan lotion that I purchased at the pool nor the countless other little amenities that I felt my prize should have included. No matter, it did cover food, lodging and libations, as well as any show at the hotel.

After I awoke from my nap, I noticed a small advertisement that beckoned from the night stand. The brochure simply stated that blondes, brunettes, redheads and other showgirls were available to "show you the town."

I suddenly realized that I could treat someone, anyone, to a sumptuous meal. Why eat alone, I asked myself, if the hotel picked up the tab?

I dialed the number. (Local calls weren't included in my prize either.) Immediately a very sultry voice replied at the other end.

I tactfully explained my situation, knowing full well that there would be countless of aspiring actresses who craved a free evening meal. After all, why not? Because, it seemed, "All our ladies are paid by the hour. You discuss with them what you want."

As much as I tried, I couldn't get my point across. And for me to spend big bucks on a dinner that supposedly was free seemed ridiculous at best.

Sometime later, I wandered downstairs, just in time for the first dinner show. In Las Vegas, if you sat through a dinner show, you really witnessed two events. The first, and more remarkable aspect for me, was observing the staff wine, dine and bus some two thousand guests in a matter of moments. How the chefs cooked, the waiters served and the busboys cleared hundreds of tables, within minutes, seemed remarkable in itself. The second spectacle, of course, was the show. Glitter, glamour and a minimum of clothes.

When one sees a show in Las Vegas, and desires a good seat, one needs to look like a big spender or at least a big tipper. I knew one gentleman who always folded his two dollar bills in such a manner that they looked like twenties. Of course he couldn't see the same show twice, but who would want to? I must have looked the part because I found myself at a perfect location.

The show proved to be spectacular. Lights, music, action, animals, magicians, choreography and beautiful dancers. Lions disappeared. Costumes flew. Ping Pong balls were juggled and the show went on.

My neighbor, between elbowing me in the midriff, alluded to the fact that this show seemed nothing. What's a disappearing lion, he asked, when they did it with elephants down the way? Perhaps he was right, but I was impressed nonetheless.

Two hours later the show finished, the lights turned brighter and everyone hustled themselves into the real action, the gambling casino. Here hundreds of aspiring millionaires played the slots, the gaming tables and Keno with sheer bravado.

My favorite game was roulette. I preferred roulette because it seemed perfect for my hidden clairvoyant talents. I closed my eyes, dreamt the next number, placed my bet and watched the ball hit a different hole. Or in those rare instances where I imagined the correct number, I didn't bet. All very confusing and certainly entertaining.

A good friend of mine had given me ten dollars for the "21"

table.

"If those ten dollars win," he had said, "leave the twenty. If the twenty wins, leave the forty. If the forty wins, take the money and run."

Much to my consternation, I won eighty bucks, which only added insult to injury as I immediately spent his eighty dollars on myself, along with all of my money. A perfect case of deficit spending in the worst possible way.

Most people who go to Las Vegas do so for the entertainment, change of scenery, sun, glamour or excitement. Few do it for gambling, per se. But most gamble.

I saw a dazzling assortment of people. Young, elderly, bushy-tailed, tired, thin, stout, happy, sad, groomed, slovenly, rich and poor, all wearing shorts, slacks, bathing suits, tuxedos, furs and every kind of real and fake, probably fake, jewelry that you could name. A very bewildering group of people, to say the least.

Nowhere can one see clocks, windows, skylights or anything which suggest the time of day. One never knows the proper time, nor if you gamble at 6:00 A.M. or 6:00 P.M. One only knows that money changes hands rapidly

Twice I attempted to play tennis but never found a partner. Most of the time the weather seemed overcast. So was my disposition.

When I finally left, my "free" hotel bill wasn't exactly free. That, coupled with my friend's eighty, (which I felt obligated to return,) plus my own money, plus Bakersfield, gas and miscellaneous, resulted in my free vacation costing over four hundred dollars.

Now what did Barnum say about a fool being born every minute? Or was Barnum the fellow that stated a man and his money soon parted company? On the other hand, who ever suggested that vacations should be free? Surely they weren't. Just buy a raffle ticket, and you'll see.

My next vacation, I decided, would be one where everything was included ahead of time. That way, nothing could go wrong. Or so I hoped.

XXVIII

Three Is A Crowd

I DECIDED TO SIGN UP FOR A CLUB MEDITERRANEAN vacation. I had heard about the various Club Meds, particularly about their carefree soirees, swinging singles and open beaches. I also heard that times had changed, and so had Club Med. Club Med had transformed itself into a Mecca for family fun. In addition, Club Med included everything for one price, an extremely important feature.

I also understood that Club Med villages existed all over the world, that life seemed good but spartan, that the Club frowned on newspapers and outside diversions and that one could drink all the wine and beer one cared for. Beyond that, I knew very little, but was relieved to know I wouldn't have to drink the water.

My destination was Playa Blanca, Mexico, a small beach front resort between Manzanilla and Puerto Vallarte. I flew there by direct charter from Los Angeles.

By the time I arrived in L.A. I began having second thoughts. Our flight would take off with a chartered plane, and my fellow-passengers looked far more mundane than the Grecian gods and goddesses I had imagined. Furthermore, our waiting line reminded me too much of basic training. But after I shared a couple of beers with my brother, who gleefully saw me off, I boarded the plane.

Three hours later we landed in Manzanilla, on a narrow runway directly parallel to the ocean. Manzanilla's new airport bustled inside with hundreds of tourists and outside with hordes of mosquitoes.

"None in Playa Blanca," promised our guide, "I assure you." Miraculously, he was right. Some time later, we climbed into three rattling busses and began the sweltering ninety minute ride to Playa Blanca. Though we couldn't see the road, we easily felt its bumps and winding turns. Occasionally, the light of a house or tiny village glimmered. Otherwise, we saw nothing. Part of a plan to hide our route I decided, and a devious one at that.

This general feeling of the unknown contributed to every passenger acquiring a common bond with his or her neighbor. Bottles of tequila worked their way up and down the aisles, and everyone quickly became friends and talked openly about themselves, their lives, their problems and why they signed up.

By now, I had made some astute observations about my fellow guests. Half were couples and the other half singles, split evenly between men and women. Each of the singles possessed two thoughts. The first dealt with the possibility of falling in love. The second concerned one's unknown roommate.

The Club matched same-sex roommates arbitrarily, with no regard to interests or habits. Consequently, the outcome might prove somewhat uncomfortable. On the other hand, as only seven days were involved, matching shouldn't have mattered that much.

Nevertheless, everyone appeared very concerned. I knew of one lady who became so paranoid about her unknown female roommate that she opted for a newly-encountered male companion, namely her seat mate on the plane.

Unfortunately, she jumped from the fat into the fire. Not only was her new-found friend far less platonic than she had anticipated, (or maybe more so, who knew?) but the club management refused to switch roommates. Only if the management made the error, and obviously this appeared to be a mistake of her own choosing.

She ultimately moved into the only room she found, that of two chivalrous men. (As I was one of those two gentlemen, I can vouch for this story.)

We arrived in Playa Blanca in style. Trumpets blew. Banners waved. Flares darted and a bevy of hosts and hostesses welcomed us with open arms and colorful drinks. Then a late dinner and a brief introduction. Then up to our rooms for some and a taste of disco for others.

Finding one's room proved difficult. Playa Blanca resembled a modern version of an ancient Portuguese village, complete with cobblestones, brick walls, tiny alleys, steep stairs and a minimum of light.

My roommate, Mike, turned out to be an affable young attorney from Southern California, and our rooms seemed adequate, though sparse. Mike went off to disco and I turned in. Midweek, when our additional roommate, Brenda, joined us, we found her just as friendly. She also proved to be a whiz in applying liberal amounts of suntan lotion every day.

On the other hand, every time we walked through our tiny foyer we had to maneuver carefully around her extensive array of personal belongings. These ranged from tennis racket and hair dryer to a six foot mattress that she and Mike had smuggled in. Playa Blanca hadn't planned on three to a room and our quarters got very cramped. But in the interest of maintaining good will, we managed admirably.

The first morning, I arose early and made a brief tour of the village. The complex housed some six hundred guests, sat between two mountains and a palm-shrouded beach and included a large dining room, theater and swimming pool. Extending in every direction, I noted tennis courts, volleyball courts, bocceball courts and broad lawns. Plenty of opportunity for exercise, that seemed certain.

Soon I ran to the beach, dove into the inviting waters and swam energetically. The ocean seemed a refreshing change from the stifling bus ride of the previous night. I did not know the time and also discovered I might be the only individual awake. No early birds in Playa Blanca.

I finally found one individual with a watch. "Do you have the time?" I asked.

"Sunday," he replied.

"Yes, I know," I said. "But what time is it, please?"

"Sunday," he replied once again.

Suddenly I knew. Time meant nothing at Playa Blanca. Nor did anyone care who you were or what you did. You could be somebody of importance or nobody. You could attempt something energetic or nothing and no one gave a hoot. Therein lay Playa Blanca's charm, its simplicity.

I also discovered that two groups of people existed. First came our hosts, the GOs, (gentil organisateurs) who seemed the ones in the know. These numbered over one hundred, appeared mostly French, in their twenties and assumed responsibility for countless activities including an amateur cabaret every evening.

GOs rotated from club to club every six months and seemed full of fun and merriment. Then came the lesser breed, the GMs (gentil memberes). These were the humble guests, like myself, and ranged in age from twenty to over sixty.

If one didn't hear the Spanish language of the chambermaids, gardeners or waiters, one could be anywhere in the world, but most likely France. One heard French spoken continuously, not only by the GOs, but also by the French Canadians, who accounted for one fourth of the guests. The remainder seemed from the United States and Europe.

At Playa Blanca, three major events occurred every day. The first and foremost was sunbathing. One could sunbathe around the pool, in the water, on the boats, on the beach, the dock or the courts. One could do so with vigor and intent or with a gentle acceptance, but in either instance one generally ended up with too much sun.

The second event, and almost as important, was the daily ritual of indulging in three square meals. The club served a breakfast and luncheon buffet and a family style dinner. One could sit anywhere with anyone and eat almost anything. During luncheon, I counted a variety of seventy dishes. Wine flowed constantly, and one learned to become an expert at opening beers with the flick of a spoon.

Finally, one danced. One danced outside or inside and listened to a live band or a disco. All night, if one wished.

The biggest game in town seemed meeting one's neighbor. One pursued this venture in numerous activities, ranging from sailing, snorkeling and scuba diving to yoga, backgammon and classical music. If one desired, one could wander over to the bar and engage in a specific libation, for which one paid in beads. On arrival, all guests checked their money and valuables at the office, but one could always charge a new string of nominally-priced beads. Bead necklaces appeared to be in haute couture at all times, with different colored beads representing different denominations of currency.

Most times, one found oneself engulfed in a daily stream of group activities, ranging from tennis round robins to marathon dance contests. We engaged in picnics and modified Olympics.

Two of the more unusual events were a body painting contest and a novel "walk on water" where guests attempted to walk a tennis net, while others tried to hold the net flat in the water. Some of these contests ended up topless, but in general I saw relatively little nudity.

In addition, most everyone behaved very properly. I did hear a few stories of questionable behavior, but really believed these stories were exactly that, merely fiction. I heard of one married woman who came to Playa Blanca with a girl-friend, in order to rendezvous with her boy friend. Her mother-in-law, suspecting foul play, alerted her son, who in turn arrived with a male friend of his own. The last I knew, all five of them graced the same table every evening and did so in style. They were guests at Playa Blanca, and guests were supposed to put up a good front.

The week passed rapidly. The weather proved perfect, the ocean calm, the guests pleasant and the wines potable. Although I didn't fall in love, I did meet some very interesting people. I also exercised more in a week than I normally did in a year and spent very little money to boot. At the same time, I decided that in the future I would take fewer vacations. Why not pursue altruistic activities, I thought. Why not stay at home, spend less money, become involved in charitable ventures and do good for others?

XXIX

Four Hundred Women

ONE MORNING MY TELEPHONE RANG. WOULD I BE willing to participate in a bachelor's auction where I would consent to be raffled off? For charity.

Throwing caution to the wind, I answered affirmatively. The auction supported two worthwhile causes, the venture sounded intriguing and well, why not? I should have known better.

I recalled an excellent biology instructor, who once taught us that everyone was worth two dollars, more or less. Now I had the opportunity to find out exactly how much more or less.

Soon a photographer came and snapped photos of me in my home, my yard and next to my dog. She then retained the best. She enlarged one copy into a giant poster to hang in the auction foyer. She included another in the auction's glossy brochure, which sold for five dollars.

The brochures also listed each bachelor's career, interests and hobbies, as well as the location of the bachelor's proposed rendezvous. Some participants pictured themselves next to their polished vehicles or planes and vowed to take their purchasers on carefree weekends to San Francisco or Lake Tahoe. Others promised spectacular dinners. One offered an elaborate evening on his boat. Another offered an all day horseback trip, followed by a sumptuous barbecue. It appeared that most of these bachelors possessed a sizable disposable income. Surely, greater than mine. No matter.

I promised to meet my new acquaintance on the night of a full moon, take her to my home for champagne, hors d'oeuvres and a Gypsy serenade and then invite her out to dinner at a well-established hotel. My former boss even offered to chauffeur, in his brand new Jaguar.

On the night of the big event, all the bachelors dressed to their teeth and met in a large hotel. I felt especially stylish, as I wore my father's elegant, though somewhat worn, coat and tails.

First we mingled with our would-be bidders and showed off our pearly teeth. Then the women disappeared into the grand ball room and we, into a small antechamber.

Soon we heard a brassy six-piece band, drowned out by the shrieks of four hundred overly enthusiastic women. We realized that the show had begun.

When the MC called our names, we slowly walked down the runway. At that moment, each of us preferred to be somewhere else. Anywhere else. But by then it was too late. On the other hand, once we heard our names called, we did everything possible to elicit the highest bid. Perhaps it was our competitive spirit. Maybe it was our personal pride. We did our best.

Some bachelors tore off their shirts and began flexing their muscles. Others somersaulted their way down the runway. I showed couth and only yodeled.

Then we listened expectantly for the bidding. In my case, I first heard two hundred dollars. Then three hundred, and gradually more. Finally, my bidding stopped at five hundred fifty.

I had hoped for more and later learned that five hundred fifty was exactly the median amount. Nor did I realize, until much later, that the lady who purchased me also had purchased four other bachelors. Somewhat avaricious, I felt, even if for a worthy cause.

After my turn, I relaxed and watched the final bidding. I should have left because at that point I suddenly lost my shirt, figuratively speaking.

A good friend of mine, a woman who came along for the auction, knew a number of bachelors. In fact, she persuaded one of them to enter.

When her friend appeared on stage, no one bid. Being a good Samaritan, she raised her hand, believing someone would bid higher. Someone did bid higher, but she forgot to lower her bidding card. Before she realized her error, she had bought her friend for four hundred dollars. Four hundred dollars that she didn't have.

Noticing her plight, a number of us came to her rescue and offered to help. She received two hundred dollars in cash and the assurances of other friends that they would reimburse her for the difference. Then she used my credit card for the rest. Suddenly, I had purchased half a bachelor. A bachelor that I did not need, did not want and for whom I ultimately never was reimbursed.

At the end, my two hundred dollars expense for this bachelor, coupled with the costs of dinner, violinist, champagne and caviar proved to be far more expensive than I had ever planned. In addition, when I finally went on my date, the lady who purchased me developed a crush on my chauffeur, the violinist drank all my champagne, and my dinner arrived cold. Obviously, not my kind of date.

Well, worse things could have happened. I might have broken my leg on the runway, received no bid or been stood up on my date. Suffice it to way, that was my last bachelor's auction. It also should have been my last charity affair whatsoever. Unfortunately, I didn't heed my own advice.

XXX

Mischievous Adventures

SOME YEARS LATER, I RECEIVED A CALL FROM THE
March of Dimes. Would I be interested in impersonating a jail-
bird? For their cause? Would I be willing to be taken to the
Embassy Suites in a Hummer, put on a striped black and white
shirt, have my photo taken and then visit the judge for sentenc-
ing? I should have said no, but I listened.

My job involved calling friends and asking them to bail me
out. All the proceeds would go to the March of Dimes. Certainly
a worthwhile cause, and I accepted. After all, what could go
wrong? They also implied that my bail would be around $300.

On the appointed day, a sheriff's car pulled up in front of my
house with two officers inside. Much to my neighbors' bewilderment one of the officers got out, handed me a warrant, slipped a
pair of plastic handcuffs on my wrists and away we drove. No
sight of a Hummer, but the officers told me I definitely would ride
in a Hummer on my return.

In the Embassy Suites, the March of Dimes had taken over a
large room full of tables, chairs and cell phones. Fellow prisoners
sat around and made their pleas. I was given a striped shirt,
placed in front of a fake jail, had my photo taken and proceeded
to the judge. The judge, a be-speckled, kindly-looking individual,
welcomed me.

"Welcome, Mr. Lehman," he said. "Have you lived in this
area a long time.?"

"Oh yes," I proudly proclaimed. "Since 1939."

"Oh is that right? My goodness, you must know more people than the mayor."

"Not quite," I modestly admitted, "but I do know a lot."

"Where do you work?" asked the judge casually.

"I'm retired," I admitted.

"How nice. Do you have any hobbies?"

"I like to travel." Immediately, the judge picked up his gavel, banged it loudly and proclaimed, "Mr. Lehman, I sentence you to a bail of $750." I winced. Obviously, the judge decided that retired travelers qualified for a larger amount.

I then found a vacant chair, picked up a telephone and went to work. I discovered that asking friends for money is neither easy nor a foregone conclusion. Even my brother suggested I would lose most of my friends, not that I had that many to begin with.

Some were not at home. Others reneged. One said it would be cheaper to send me a carrot cake with a file in it. Another suggested that I would have to call only 749 more friends. And so it went.

Some individuals did make $100 pledges. One even pledged more although most pledged considerably less. Without these generous souls, I still would be in jail. At the end of the afternoon, by pleading, cajoling and begging, I had raised $845. I was thrilled, and so was everyone else.

Then came time for my personal reward....a ride home in a Hummer. A National Guardsman picked me up, and away we went. I then realized that a ride in a Hummer was not as great as it first appeared. Even if Arnold Scharzenegger owned one. The seats seemed hard as a rock. There was little room. The springs tight and the noise stifling. But I did get my desire, even if I did crave to sit in a tub of ice afterwards.

I also decided that this would be the last time I would volunteer for jail. In fact, for anything. Any future charity would have only one designee and that would be me. In this manner, I might recoup some of the losses that I had been incurring

One way of bringing extra money into the coffers, I decided, was to become a professional dog sitter. I occasionally rented out my house. Now I could dog sit at the same time. In that way, I would have my cake and eat it too. With hardly a backward glance, I planned to dog sit.

XXXI

Never Sit Your Neighbor's Dog

I DECIDED TO SIT DOGS ONE SUMMER AFTERNOON after I had rented out my house without a place to go. I put an ad into the newspapers, seeking a position as a house sitter. One person answered my ad. She was a professional pet sitter and not only had one house to watch, but a number of them and their pets. Would I be interested? Of course!

Rose had come from the East Coast to be near her daughter. Overnight, she decided to become a professional dog sitter, and within a year she had cornered the market. She cornered the market by hiring responsible individuals and by being extremely conscientious. She answered my ad and fired a series of questions at me.

"Was I bondable?" I was.

"Did I like animals?" I did.

"Did I have transportation?" Yes

"Did I like to walk?" Affirmative.

"Would I be able to stay nights?" Would I! That was my reason for writing the ad in the first place. Surely I needed a roof. And Rose even offered to pay. What more could I ask for?

Soon I found out. Within the space of a month, I cared for dogs, cats and rabbits, slept in mansions, cottages and bungalows and learned that when it came to animals, each had its own needs, disposition and habits.

Rose developed a thorough questionnaire for every animal. Name, age, sex and vet seemed only the beginning. Peculiarities, such as special medicines and foods, as well as the names of neighbors and emergency numbers were all carefully noted. In fact, there was very little missing, and every dog sitter became extremely knowledgeable about his or her charges.

Nevertheless, theory and practice were not necessarily the same. Knowing how to open a particular dog's mouth, insert a pill, clamp the mouth shut until he swallowed it, and doing so without losing your hand (no butter or liverwurst for this animal) were not exactly a piece of cake.

Not allowing a certain cat to slip out when you didn't even know where the cat hid, proved just as challenging. One dog had to be watched especially carefully as he had been kidnapped once before. And miraculously found, only moments before the owners returned from a long vacation. Although that happened to another sitter, the dog, Rose, and I became slightly paranoid.

Another dog had the distinct ability to relieve herself in the middle of her owner's carpet, regardless of how often the dog went for walks. I learned to accept this idiosyncrasy, too.

My worst horror story occurred one bright and cheery morning. I walked down the owner's driveway, picked up the newspaper and then prepared to take my charge for his customary walk. The dog I sat was a beautiful Golden Retriever, bright, strong and full of spirit. He also had the reputation for barking throughout the night, and so I was to place him inside his kennel, inside the garage, before I went to bed.

The owner had shown me the garage, the kennel and the lock. She showed me everything during daylight, and I didn't think of asking about the light switch. When I retired, I couldn't find the switch, groped my way through the darkened garage, placed the dog in his kennel, checked the lock and went to bed.

The next morning, shortly after I retrieved the paper, I opened the side door to the garage and discovered that bedlam had ensued. I hadn't locked the kennel properly, and my charge had unfastened his lock, opened the gate and run berserk. In this case, with a fifty pound sack of snail pellets that now lay strewn all over the garage floor.

In the middle of this mess sat my dog, proudly. Next to him were tiny bits of paper, shredded into a thousand pieces. One of them, the largest, was still identifiable and clearly stated: "WARNING, CAN BE FATAL TO CHILDREN AND ANIMALS IF SWALLOWED."

I went nuts, grabbed the dog, pulled him into the house, seized the phone and desperately tried to call the vet. But at seven A.M., the vet wasn't in. Could he call me back? But he didn't. Or at least, he didn't in the next thirty seconds. I called the vet's office again, told them that I would meet the vet there, grabbed the dog once more, jumped into my car and off we went.

At any time of the day many highways seem slow. With an emergency and a possible suicide in the back seat, crawl seemed a better word. Every few seconds I glanced into the rear view mirror, checked my patient, and hurried on.

As invalids went, he looked pretty good. In fact, he seemed to relish the ride and presumably his predicament. On the other hand, any moment could be his last, and so, with my emergency lights flashing and one hand on the horn, I raced on. My destination was five miles distance, and every traffic light seemed red. What did I expect?

Finally, I made it into the vet's office, whipped open the car door, picked up the poor animal and flew into the waiting room. The attendants were ready. I felt like an expectant mother.

Immediately, I was subjected to a barrage of questions:

"How many pellets did he eat?" Who knew?

"How long ago?" Good question.

"Has he acted peculiarly?" Didn't he always?

"What kind of pellets?" Fortunately I held the wrapper.

And while listening to my feeble responses, the doctor prepared to pump him out or at least induce him to vomit. I was released and told to call back in a few hours.

I returned to the house and began making a series of anguishing telephone calls. To Rose. To the owner. To the vet. Then the owners called the vet. Then I called the owners. Then the owners called me back. Then they called Rose. On and on. Finally, after an eternity, and my tenth call to the vet, he assured me all was OK. My patient seemed fine, and I could pick him up shortly.

Apparently, the dog never had swallowed any pellets at all. Rather, he only played with the bag and with me. Probably, when he first heard the sound of my feet on the driveway. By this time, of course, the dog was no longer the patient. I was.

Two days later the owners returned. I bid the dog adieu and the next day began my next assignment. This time, I checked all premises first for any sign of snail pellets. I felt that one bag in a lifetime seemed more than enough.

I also decided that being a professional dog sitter was not my cup of tea. I elected to pursue other cash-inviting possibilities. As a starter, I could play Santa. For a fee. Or I might sell some of my junk on E-bay. My brother always pleaded, "Hans, please don't get run over by a truck." Why not do him a favor and get rid of some of my stuff at the same time? And I could write.

Of course, if I wrote, I wasn't guaranteed any remuneration. My funds might move in the wrong direction. Or not come in at all. But for the time being, I decided to write. What did I have to lose, other than my reputation and some more money, both of which weren't on that solid footing in the first place.

And if writing didn't work out? I guess I would have to cross that bridge later. This week, I became obsessed with writing. Next week? Who knew?

HOW TO LOSE FRIENDS
And Other Social Graces

by Hans Lehmann

AT YOUR BOOKSTORE OR FROM THE AUTHOR

Please send me:

HOW TO LOSE FRIENDS
And Other Social Graces

ISBN 1-877809-90-x

Number of books _____ @ $9.95 each   = _____

Sales Tax (add 7% for books shipped to CA)   = _____

Shipping/Handling (add $4 per book)   = _____

Add $1 for each add'l book to same address   = _____

Total Enclosed   = _____

Check or money order payable to Hans Lehmann

Send to (please print)

Name _____

Address _____

City _____

State, Zip _____

Send your payment with the order form above to:
Hans Lehmann, P.O. Box 1673, Carmel, CA 93921
Books shipped immediately upon receipt of order.

COMMENTS: _____
_____
_____

About The Author

Photo by Gary M. Russell

Hans Lehmann was born in Germany and immigrated to the United States in 1939, at the age of seven. He attended various schools and universities throughout the country, including the Webb School for Boys, the University of Colorado, and Harvard University where he received his MBA. He also served in the United States Army in Pirmasens, Germany.

From 1961 until 1989, Lehmann worked for Macy's California, where he held various management positions, including buyer. He retired as the operations manager and assistant store manager of Macy's Monterey.

In addition to a venturesome spirit and a penchant for mischievous behavior, Lehmann has always been involved in a myriad of extracurricular activities. These include traveling to remote areas, playing his concertina, hosting foreigners, playing Santa, helping charities, hiking, camping, and writing. He has published fourteen stories in the *San Jose Mercury News*, the *Monterey Herald*, and the *Carmel Pine Cone*. Some of these stories are contained in *How to Lose Friends and Other Social Graces*. This is his first book.

Lehmann lives in Carmel-by-the-Sea, California, with his Border Collie, Tippy. In 2001, he received a Volunteer Community Service Award in Monterey County for his work with the Alzheimer's Association, and was one of five Unsung Heroes in Carmel-by-the-Sea.